# THE AFTERWARDS

## BROKEN DAUGHTERS: MADE BY BROKEN FATHERS

BY

ALEX JONES

# THE AFTERWARDS
## BROKEN DAUGHTERS: MADE BY BROKEN FATHERS

ALEX JONES

THE AFTERWARDS
BROKEN DAUGHTERS: MADE BY BROKEN FATHERS

# Table of Contents

ALEX JONES

4

## THE AFTERWARDS
### BROKEN DAUGHTERS: MADE BY BROKEN FATHERS

**ALEX JONES**

# THE AFTERWARDS
## BROKEN DAUGHTERS: MADE BY BROKEN FATHERS

If you have read The Afterwards and The Afterwards: Broken Mothers of Broken Daughters made by Broken Fathers, you will know that Alex's story is based on true events. Author Alex Jones testified at her father's trial against her mother's wishes and against the biddings of her family.

Even though he was found guilty of his crimes against Alex and her sisters, he was never sentenced to prison followings Alex's, who was fifteen at the time, desperate pleas to the court to secure his freedom.

The judge in the case issued a lifetime restraining order against him to refrain from any contact with his daughters but were ignored by both her parents.

To allow the author's family protection, character names are fictitious.

*Any resemblance to actual persons, living or dead, is entirely coincidental.*

**ALEX JONES**

# THE AFTERWARDS
## BROKEN DAUGHTERS: MADE BY BROKEN FATHERS

ALEX JONES

# DEAR BROKEN DAUGHTER

This is the part of my journey where I speak about you and hopefully, to you. I hope that after reading this, you will realize that the abuse you suffered was never your fault, and that speaking out was the right and only thing you could do.

I know you are trying to overcome and accept your scars, your fight and your pain. I know you feel guilty about surviving, and I hope I can teach you to celebrate your victory.

I know that you have spent every moment since you found your voice to choose right over wrong, even when others didn't. I know you get up and show up each day, even though you'd rather crawl into a hole, and live there forever.

I know you are clinging to a life that has let you down, that confuses you, that has betrayed you, and that has desperately disappointed you. I know you are holding on for dear life. I know that you sometimes can't breathe when the waves of sorrow come crashing down on you. I know you are trying to find your place in a broken world, filled with broken people. I know you force a smile when all you really want to do is cry. I know how much you hate yourself each time you look in the mirror, unable to find a reason to love yourself.

I know you are trying, even when no-one else can see it. I am trying too. I am with you. Believe only this if you can believe nothing else.

If you had told me a week before I woke up different that I would be stronger, braver, and determined to banish my monsters back into the abyss, this time without me and my sisters, I would never have believed you.

I was afraid, I was complicit, I thought I was loved, but more than anything, I loved the boogeyman. One morning, I woke up different, and so will you.

You will be removed from those against you when you figure out who those are that serve you. You will no longer care about those who watch from the sidelines, unable to commit to picking a side. Those that pretend not to know, not to hear, and not to see. You will discard all that no longer offers you peace. You will value your opinion more – others won't matter so much.

Your only validation will come from you, no-one else. Loyalty will first be for you. You will reclaim the you that was once

# THE AFTERWARDS
## BROKEN DAUGHTERS: MADE BY BROKEN FATHERS

stolen from you, and from the world. You will reclaim your heart, body, mind and soul. You will eventually reclaim your joy and your happiness. You will ultimately reclaim that inner you that was stolen by the monsters of your days and of your nights.

More than anything, for the remainder of your life, you will remember that you were called to a war, many others weren't. Perhaps you've seen too much. Perhaps you've felt too much and been through more than you should have. Perhaps, you've been asked too much of, and perhaps, you've lost too much of yourself along the way. I am here to tell you that all the too-much'es can never dim your beauty, your strength and your you'ness. You will find your way, because despite the too-much'es, you are still here. You are chosen because of the too-much'es, others would never have survived.

It happened to you; it isn't you. It doesn't define you and it will never be who you are. Their truth will never be your truth. You are grace.

Alex :D<

# THE AFTERWARDS
## BROKEN DAUGHTERS: MADE BY BROKEN FATHERS

ALEX JONES

THE AFTERWARDS
BROKEN DAUGHTERS: MADE BY BROKEN FATHERS

# FROM THE AUTHOR

My name is Alex. I am a wife and mother of two. I am also one third of three daughters which means, I am missing two thirds of me. But today, here and now, that's okay. I have learnt to live with their absence, and I am on an unbelievable, inspiring, better-than-before journey that has led to all things amazing.

God found me and showed me my fight. One that would take me to war, leaving many casualties in its wake. But, it was also a war that made me braver than I ever was, and stronger than I could ever have imagined I'd be.

When I began writing about this, my notes were intended for letters to me, and turned out to be one of the hardest things I have ever had to do. Each time I would put pen to paper, emotions I had locked down a long time ago, were opened up.

It left me feeling softer, and so much more vulnerable than I would have liked to feel. But, at the same time, it kept me going, and as I re-read the tear-stained letters to myself, I was

ALEX JONES

# THE AFTERWARDS
## BROKEN DAUGHTERS: MADE BY BROKEN FATHERS

reminded of what I fought for. At times, it was hard to feel the way I would feel, and it's never the same the next time.

In the end, it was a war we had been called to, that others would never know of.

Life isn't always about roses and butterflies. Days are filled with ups and downs, but I focus on all the brilliance in my life, and I count my blessings each day.

You can too.

ALEX JONES

# Copyright 2019

# The Afterwards:

## Broken Daughters - Made by Broken Fathers

# Alex Jones

ALEX JONES

# THE AFTERWARDS
## BROKEN DAUGHTERS: MADE BY BROKEN FATHERS

ALEX JONES

# BROKEN DAUGHTER

I hope today is the day you realize that it was never your fault. For so long, broken daughters live with a kind of culpability we are trapped and caged in.

Initially, we blame ourselves for the abuse and sexual deprivations of our monsters or boogeymen. We question the way we look, the way we dress, the way we walk, talk, and sit. We question each hug and kiss. We question our attitude and what we might have said to lure us into the boogeyman's web.

We then berate ourselves for speaking out or confiding in someone. We take on the responsibilities of our families falling apart, our mother or father's heartache, the pain of our brothers or sisters, but, more than anything, we blame ourselves for speaking out.

We end up trying to take it all back. Trying to find anything to tell us that we were wrong. We analyze and dissect each and every moment with our abusers, trying to find reasons

ALEX JONES

# THE AFTERWARDS
## BROKEN DAUGHTERS: MADE BY BROKEN FATHERS

to justify their behavior. We question whether it was truly abuse, and if it was truly as horrific as we once thought it was.

Perhaps, you begin punishing yourself in a desperate effort to numb the guilt which causes a kind of pain almost worse than the abuse, and worse than the pain you feel when you consider the emotions of the abuser, and all those who love him.

You begin asking yourself questions so as to have reasons to punish and hurt yourself. Perhaps, sex wasn't the end goal in your abusive situation, so you question whether it was truly sexual abuse when there was no sex? Yes, it was. You were too young, too ignorant, or too complicit as a result of fear, to be able to say no. If it made you uncomfortable and fearful, it was sexual abuse. The fact that your abuser is your father, or another family member means that it was abuse. They should never have placed you in a position where intimacy was even considered. And even if you did say no, it wouldn't have mattered. It rarely will stop the abuse before it starts or end it after it begins. Because there was no intercourse, does not mean that you weren't physically and emotionally abused.

Sexual abuse was a secret you had to keep, no matter what. Keeping a secret such as that for someone hurting you, confirms the fact that your abuser is in the wrong, and that it is a crime.

Because you were perhaps seeking attention from your abuser, or because you sat on his lap or flung your arms around him, even if your dresses were short and your shorts were tight, does not make it your fault. It was not an invitation to violate you.

Your abuser was someone you trusted, and in the case of a father, someone you loved and worshipped. He was someone you thought would love and protect you from being subjected to any kind of abuse. He was the very first man you loved.

Even if the physical abuse wasn't as painful or traumatic, the emotional scars are worse than the physical force you've had to endure. Threatening you, blaming you, cautioning you, and making you keep his secret is often the worst kind of abuse for most child sexual abuse survivors.

Because he was drunk or high when he targeted you, doesn't excuse his failure to keep you safe and unharmed. Remember that most fathers who consume large amounts of alcohol or use drugs on a regular basis, never abuse their daughters. It is choices they make, choices you never had a say in. Even if speaking out afterwards will anger your father, get him into trouble with the law, remove your father from your family, anger your mother, or perhaps no-one will believe you, it is never a reason to be silenced. The fact that you told someone means that you are fighting for your life, and your survival.

You must and finding one person who will believe in and support you, is the first step you could ever take to finding yourself again, letting go of the past, and creating a beautiful life for yourself without your boogeyman in it.

Because you have been sexually abused, does not mean you will never trust anyone again.

It doesn't mean you will never love again, and it doesn't mean you will never have normal again.

Your you'ness is unique, precious, and special. It is you, and all you face and overcome on your journey in this world.

The emotions that will take you on a rollercoaster ride will leave you second-guessing yourself, and your motives for speaking out, but the reasons you didn't speak out right at the beginning is why you must believe that The Afterwards you find yourself in, was never your fault. You carried your cross because you were too afraid to speak out. You were afraid of your abuser's anger and threats. You were afraid that no-one would believe you. You were in disbelief that it actually happened, and then you wondered if it was in fact, wrong.

The shame you feel for being unable to stop it, isn't your shame to bare. It is your abuser's, and anyone else who actively knew, or participated in the abuse. Your anger is justified, and you have a right to confront your abuser. He was supposed to protect you. He didn't.

If you are confused by all that had happened to you, you might want to find the answers to the why's, the how-could-he's and the destruction he brought into your lives. Speaking out does not mean you betrayed your abuser. By sexually abusing you, he betrayed you, your family and the world. Talking about what you have been through gives you the strength to become healthy again. It lets you see yourself the way those who love you do.

Make the decision to love yourself again by realizing that you are a survivor of a war others will never be called to.

It's a daily struggle to work through the memories of before and afterwards. Don't let your heartbreak leave you feeling stupid and sad for trusting someone not to hurt you. Talk about your story as though it is your life's greatest accomplishment because your survival will always be what will stand out about you.

ALEX JONES

You were never to blame for what happened to you. It happened to you, and can never define who you were, who you are today, and you become tomorrow. You didn't deserve what happened, no matter how often you try to convince yourself that you had a role in initiating the abuse. You didn't.

Break down those walls for those who want to walk with you through your afterwards. Keep your abuser and those who defend his actions, on the other side of you.

Be patient with your recovery. Hold on to your authenticity. It was never your fault, and it can never become your fault. Don't try to understand your abuser. Don't make excuses for him. Don't try and convince yourself that you didn't have a right to a life without the abuse in it. You did. You do.

Don't withdraw blame from those who knew and did nothing to help you. Whether you were a child, a teenager, or a young adult, you had a right to be loved and protected. Cast your shame aside.

What happened to you was shameful, but it is not your shame. If others close to you avoid the truth or avoid acknowledging your abuse because it might be too traumatic to hear, remember that you lived it.

ALEX JONES

## THE AFTERWARDS
### BROKEN DAUGHTERS: MADE BY BROKEN FATHERS

You had no choice or say in it. You were never afforded the privilege to sidestep it simply because it was too traumatic to live it. You were denied your voice and you lived, what they can barely imagine. Some will say that they aren't ready to hear this, and they might be who you need the most, but nobody really knows much about what happened to you, but you, not even your abuser. He has no idea what he put you through, or what your suffering was like. It was about him, his needs, and his perverted desires. It was never about you.

You have finally found your voice, and it can never be silenced again. Speak out and let those around you know that as much as they are not ready to hear it, you were never ready to live it. But remember, as closely as your story will play out in their minds, they will never truly understand or comprehend that, that you were forced to endure. The value you place on your silence is so much greater than speaking up. You are wrong. Surviving is about speaking up, even if your voice trembles and shudders. As much as your healing might be accelerated by professionals trained to deal with your story, it is imperative that you identify your feelings and what you view as your part in the abuse.

Un-teach yourself all your abuser taught you and do it your way. Grab onto the hands trying to help you up, and turn your back on an afterwards that is harsh, cruel, unkind,

ALEX JONES

# THE AFTERWARDS
## BROKEN DAUGHTERS: MADE BY BROKEN FATHERS

destructive and lacking of what you need. Storms will rage from time to time, and rain will come crashing down on you every now and again. But instead of drowning, swim. Instead of hiding from the rain, dance in it. Sunlight is on the horizon. Your life in The Afterwards is not set in stone, and changes constantly. Find your wonderful there. Grab a hold of promises for a better life there, and tailor-make it to be everything you had ever dreamed of.

Discard those terrifying threats your boogeyman once whispered in your ear. Abolish the tears that only came out at night. Don't run. Don't hide. Don't come undone, and don't cast your feelings aside. Let go of the secrets you could never speak of. Close the gateway to the hell you were living in. You have nothing to be sorry for. You have nothing to fear anymore.

Crawl if you have to. You will walk soon enough. It was never your fault. The shame is not yours to live with, but the sickness of someone else's soul. You are not defective or corrupt.

Carrying shame and feelings of guilt around with you, prolongs the power your boogeyman had over you. Have compassion for yourself and understand that you have lost as much as everyone else involved has. Your life ahead no longer has to be terrifying or rotten with guilt on your behalf. Your speaking out must never become your greatest sadness.

ALEX JONES

# THE AFTERWARDS
## BROKEN DAUGHTERS: MADE BY BROKEN FATHERS

You have permission to be human, and to survive. You won't get things right the first time, every time, but that's alright. Bad things don't simply happen to people because they are below average, or poor, or have had an average upbringing. It's not because perhaps, parents are uneducated, jobless, or even homeless. Bad things don't target the less wealthy or the less known. The train rolls, and it won't matter on which side of the tracks you are from. Yesterday is a story for another day, for someone else to tell, because you are different now.

Yesterday, is a memory to conjure up, only to serve as a reminder of your victory. Yesterday was a promise of your dream today. Today, you are different than yesterday, and different to who you'll be tomorrow.

Life gets simpler and easier. Give yourself as many peaceful days as you need. Wear your wings and fly away if you must. Put on your crown even if there are thorns. Be brave enough to cherish yourself. It's your story. It's your yesterday, today and tomorrow. You'll be different through them all. Where you've walked yesterday, where you walk today and where you will walk tomorrow, none have walked before.

ALEX JONES

# THE AFTERWARDS
## BROKEN DAUGHTERS: MADE BY BROKEN FATHERS

ALEX JONES

# GRIEVE AND BREATHE

When I moved into the next phase of my life, after I had spoken out about the abuse and into the first days of The Afterwards, all I was aware of was the aftermath and destruction left behind by my boogeyman. Somehow, it made me feel that it was left behind by me, and as punishment for turning my father in. I felt awful and couldn't see that it wasn't my fault. I couldn't forgive myself for all that was lost as a result of speaking out.

I experienced humiliation at a level I had never known before, and I felt powerless that I was unable to stop my father before anyone discovered the abuse. I was sorely aware of what every single member of my family had lost, especially my father, who had temporarily lost his freedom.

But not once did I consider the fact that I had lost just as much as they did. I was betrayed and hurt by my father, the first man I had ever loved. It left me reeling and feeling that I had missed out on a normal childhood, and that my family unit was now in shards. I buried my own grief by blaming myself for the grieving of everyone else, and as a result, I applied dishonor to myself. I told myself that I had no right to grieve my losses since I turned him in. I believed that my grief was false, and denied it to myself for many, many years. But what I didn't realize was that I owed it to myself to process my own heartache and losses.

I had a right to mourn the trauma I had suffered. Not only did I lose a life that could have been different had the abuser not infiltrated my innocence, but so too, did I lose confidence in those closest to me, and the remainder of the world when I stepped into The Afterwards.

While the abuse was taking place, I lost my freedom, but more crushingly, I lost my identity. My identity was altered the moment my boogeyman slapped an 'abused-child' label on me. It changed me from a carefree child who knew nothing about boogeymen and monsters into one that suddenly only knew fear, guilt, shame, heartache, and abhorrence.

My identity had been altered both during the abuse and later in The Afterwards. In order to be kind to myself, I had to grieve who I had become in order to discard all the labels that were placed on me and reclaim the pieces of my me'ness. My freedom was stolen from me each time my father silenced me and swore me to secrecy. By placing such a tremendous responsibility on me, he was effective in caging me, and keeping me imprisoned for years to come. In the process, I lost my ability to trust anyone. I had enormous faith in my father, the man I once thought would give his life to defending and protecting me.

Without the ability to trust anyone at all, the world became a whole lot more challenging than when I was able to trust those I thought would care for me.

Without a doubt, these losses led to feelings of abandonment, brokenness, numbness, and irreparable damage to all I thought I knew. It contradicted all I was ever taught, and all I thought was valuable, and cherished.

During the early days of The Afterwards, the numbness I was feeling was a welcome escape to the disbelief that had crept up on me. The temporary detachment from my emotions mercifully dimmed my excruciating heartache. For the first time since the abuse began, I realized that I had no understanding whatsoever of what really happened to me, and what the consequences were once my boogeyman was exposed. For a while, it left me feeling paralyzed by the horror and anxiety I was experiencing.

It was only when I embraced the fact that I was not responsible or at fault for the decisions, actions, and subsequent consequences of my father's choices, that I was able to look at myself with a little more kindness. I was once carefree, happy and still nothing more than a child. What was once a safe haven for me, had turned into the epicenter of my nightmares. I lost the ability to sleep at night without watching the door handle turn during the abuse, and later, without the nightmares that were taunting me and convincing me that it wasn't yet over.

I would fall asleep listing for sounds to warn me of my boogeyman, and later, the silence scared me even more. There was nothing peaceful about going to sleep at night, instead, it left me feeling chaotic, restless, and fidgety when an unfamiliar sound would wake me.

I was no longer able to walk down a street without looking over my shoulders anymore. I expected a boogeyman or monster around every corner and turn. I was convinced that he would find me again and unleash his wrath on me.

In The Afterwards, I was painfully aware of the stares and whispers from my immediate and extended family. I had lost the way I once functioned in my family, and the way they knew me before 'the thing;' before the abuse.

This made way for feelings of denial, and left me questioning once again, whether the abuse actually took place

BROKEN DAUGHTERS: MADE BY BROKEN FATHERS

and whether it was as bad as I thought it was. At times, I would find myself in a state of shock, and conjure up the most unrealistic thoughts my mind allowed me to. One such thought was, what if I was the one who had imagined it all? What if it never really happened, and I had turned an innocent man in? What if it was a figment of my imagination, and that I was mentally impaired? What if I belonged in a mental institution? I lost the ability to trust myself.

I was grieving and trying to make sense of how we got to where we were. I felt bouts of depression and anxiety overwhelm me each moment I spent trying to identify the turmoil within. The sadness I was feeling initially increased drastically, and my determination to survive was lost.

I was overcome with feelings of loneliness, hopelessness, anger and despair, and in turn, it stole my ability to exonerate myself not only for desperately trying to survive the abuse, but for tearing my family apart.

Grieving for what my family had lost, was as excruciating and debilitating as grieving the loss of someone who had died. I was grieving a life and a time without boogeymen and monsters. I was grieving the me that was free of shame and guilt, and I was harshly berating myself for exposing my father to the world. I was

ALEX JONES

able to remain silent about the abuse, because my father threatened a fate far worse than the abuse in itself. I lost the ability to open up about my feelings, and later, expressing my emotions and grieving my losses.

I lost my innocence, my childhood, parents, the stability and security that I once knew, but more than anything else, I lost the ability to love myself. I grieved for a life we could have had, had the abuse not taken place. I longed for the father he could have been, had he not been overrun by his own demons. I longed for the family unit we were before my father was replaced with a beast, out to destroy my childhood. I went into The Afterwards with undeniable emptiness and overwhelming sorrow for the person I might have been, had the abuse never occurred.

In the early days, I wandered around aimlessly in The Afterwards, barely making sense of my own grief. I immersed myself in feelings of self-sabotage, self-blame, and constant bereavement. I was reluctant to concede to the fact that it was the boogeyman's disgrace, and not mine. It was his indignity that allowed my degradation, and in the process, brought up immense self-reproach at the grief I was experiencing for all we had lost in the process. During the abuse, I lost all hope and most of my faith. I was faced with invisible barriers that rocked the very foundation I was built on. I lost myself and for a moment, I lost

# THE AFTERWARDS
## BROKEN DAUGHTERS: MADE BY BROKEN FATHERS

the belief that God would draw the line. I lost faith that we would be rescued. I lost my voice, and all the memories of all that was once good in my life. I lost my self-worth, and in its place, I was desperately trying to deal with feelings of immense blame. I grieved silently and where no-one else could see. It was, after all, all my fault.

Healing from my grief did not happen overnight and is different for us all. I often revisited much of what I lost in an attempt to get it back.

I needed to recapture the ability to trust in order to build an intimate relationship, and I needed to evoke my self-worth, to raise children in a functional and stable environment.

After three decades of healing, I understand that I might need to grieve certain aspects of the abuse and The Afterwards forever, but moving forward did happen, and in my own time. Grief often springs unexpected feelings of anger on me when I am reminded with the reality that someone I loved, betrayed me, stole my innocence from me, and then, for leaving me with a messy and muddled heart.

Forgiving myself and in order to process my grief meant that I had to force myself to accept the fact that I was harmed without provoking the attacks and abuse. I would often be overcome with rage and resentment towards not only my father, but towards those who knew, and especially my mother who failed to step up for us.

It opened up a door for me to confront them, and in the process, I was able to take back the power they stripped from me. It gave me permission to become louder, and in turn, I silenced them.

My anger was mainly focused on my mother and the fact that she refused to help us. Our secrets could have remained a secret, and the world would never have to know about it. Instead, as a result of losing my mother's willingness to safeguard us, I was responsible for speaking out, and putting an end to the abuse my sisters and I were suffering. It was placed on my shoulders. It was left up to me. I was charged with saving us, and I hated that.

My family was not ready to hear that my father was our boogeyman, and as a result, I not only lost both my parents, but my sisters and extended family in the process. Dealing with the grief of losing faith in my mother has allowed me to exonerate her for missing the signs of 'the thing,' but as quickly as I did, I unforgave her for losing her in The Afterwards. I blamed her for choosing the life my father had given her, over a life without the

ALEX JONES

beatings and abuse. I blamed her for holding me responsible for the abuse, speaking out, and our losses. I grieved immensely over her denial of the monster that lurked inside our home.

It was only once I realized that I couldn't fix her, but that it was never my responsibility to, that I was able to deal with losing her, allowing me to grieve losing all the rest.

One day, I looked back and realized that my life was a big deal, and that I should have been told that. Perhaps it wasn't important to my parents or to the rest of the world, but it was to me. I often reflect on the days I felt worthless when trying to make myself so small so as to hide myself from the world, and I realize how monumental I was in overcoming all that was trying to destroy me. I sometimes linger in the breaths I struggled to inhale, and they become extraordinary to me.

For all the days that I thought I was never enough, I realize now how significant I was. That was my first step to creating a life I would never need to run away from.

I paid closer attention to my heart and the road it wanted to take me on when I realized it knew the way. I lost much, but like you, I am a miracle. Be softer and kinder to yourself and be present in your now. Put aside your past and the grief you've had to process and overcome. It was never your fault. It was never

ALEX JONES

anything you did, said or dressed yourself in. It was never your job to solve the demons of your abuser, and those who were complicit in the abuse.

It was never up to you to save yourself. You should never have been placed in that position in the first place. Avoid that which causes you to grieve again. Give yourself permission to say no. Allow yourself to love yourself again. Follow your dreams and make yourself your first priority. End all that is toxic in your life, even if it is a mother or a father. Stand up for yourself and know that you have nothing to be ashamed of. Again, the guilt is not yours to carry. It never, ever was.

Love your imperfections and flaws. Demand respect and banish those who don't value you. Set boundaries with anyone that fails to serve you or promote peace in your life. Slow down and sit quietly. Rummage through the chaos that appears every now and again. Find yourself and call back your you'ness.

Your innocence may have died, but you didn't. Believe that whatever is hurting you, will heal. Don't hide your pain. Don't pretend that you're coping. Take your time and manage all you need to so that you can find your way to your village where a pack of wolves is waiting to show you a kind of love that is healthy and kind. Walk away from that which weighs heavily on

# THE AFTERWARDS
## BROKEN DAUGHTERS: MADE BY BROKEN FATHERS

you and walk away from those who ignite feelings of guilt and shame in you. If I can tell you anything today, it is that you are important, you are needed, you are extraordinary, you matter and you are good enough.

Go home to your village, your you'ness by forgiving yourself, and find your wonderful. Find your tribe that sees your value and worth. Go home to your village, where you will find the peace you are so desperately hunting, the joy you are so fraught to feel again, and the love you deserve just as much as anyone else does.

Step out of that, that almost destroyed you. May I remind you that you are amazing in all the battles you are fighting. You are a warrior like no other. You are beautiful. You are special. How many could have survived the war you were called to? Forgive yourself for the guilt that was never yours. Grieve. It is yours to embrace and forgive yourself for allowing it.

ALEX JONES

# THE AFTERWARDS
## BROKEN DAUGHTERS: MADE BY BROKEN FATHERS

ALEX JONES

# ANGER TO SADNESS TO ANGER

When I reflect back to the years of abuse, and then to the first few years in The Afterwards, I can barely deny the fact that I was angry for so many different reasons, and at so many different people. What I struggled to understand, was that I was angry all the time, and mostly, at myself.

I was angry, and sad. It was a kind of broken rage that was conquered by the tremendous hurt I was feeling for everyone else. I was angry at myself for 'allowing' the abuse. Then, I was angry that I couldn't stop it. I was angry that I had remained silent for years, labelling myself as a coward in the process. I was angry at myself for wearing short dresses and skirts. I was angry at myself for sitting on my father's lap. I was angry at myself for the way I looked and acted. There was nothing about me that I didn't hate.

Later, I was angry at myself for speaking out and turning my father in. I was angry that I had the audacity to accuse him of abuse and splitting up our family in the process. I was angry at

ALEX JONES

myself for temporarily putting my father in prison. I was angry at myself for being the reason my mother experienced immeasurable heartache at not only losing her husband, but her entire life. She lost everything.

I was angry at myself for being the source of my sisters' heartache, and my extended family's withdrawal from us. I was angry for the decisions I made, and for following through with them.

Each time my mother pointed out that my sadness was an act, it brought out a kind of rage for myself, I had never known before. But, what nobody told me was that my anger was justified, just not antagonism and resentment towards myself.

I was exhausted by the grief my mother experienced losing my father, her home and most of her personal belongings. She spent much time reflecting on all she had lost, and how painful it was to start over again, and against her will. Her pining for my father, a man that assaulted her a hundred times before, was what initiated my initial anger towards her. Her grief was never for us, and what we went through. It was purely for what she had lost.

My anger for her escalated rapidly when I realized that she was so blinded by her grief, that she failed to consider the fact that we were grieving too. The fact that she took out her anger on me for taking 'matters' into my own hands, angered me all the more.

The resentment I felt while listening to her criticize me and my desperation to survive, was a kind of anger I welcomed, and valued. I allowed myself to feel it, even though she would at first, never see it. I thought I needed punishment, and I thought I would feel better afterwards.

The anger I felt for her was what ultimately convinced me to no longer apologize to her for hurting her, my father and our family. My intense rage for her was the beginning of interrupting years of dysfunction that opened my eyes to a reality that it was never my fault.

Because of my infuriation of her, I was able to distance myself from, and free myself from my role in splitting up our family. It was as though she had handed me a key to free myself from a cage I had been locked in for years.

The anger I felt for her during the first years in The Afterwards, was so much more intense than the anger I felt for her during 'the thing.' I cherish and value my anger for her, and even though it has given me the ability to forgive her, it has also given me the choice of changing my mind, and to unforgive her.

ALEX JONES

# THE AFTERWARDS
## BROKEN DAUGHTERS: MADE BY BROKEN FATHERS

It was never that I wasn't willing to let go of my anger for her, it was that my anger for her protected me from her ability to harm me in later years. There were times that I would feel immeasurable anger towards her when it came to the little things, and other times, I would feel nothing.

I am wary to let go of my resentment of her and her inability to have saved us when we needed it. Even more so, I have forgiven myself for dragging around unfinished anger for the fact that she has never shown remorse or forgiven me for her anger in the way that she believes she was the true victim, and the one who lost everything.

Her condemnation of me in The Afterwards remains a sore point, and something I forgave, and unforgave almost immediately. I am reminded by the fact that she let it happen, after I told her. She chose him over our safety, and her own. She allowed him to beat her, and then she allowed him to not only beat us all, but to sexually abuse my sisters and I.

I am reminded of the cruelty that awaited me in The Afterwards. I remember the blame. I remember the accusations, and I remember that she admitted to never loving me. More than anything, I remember the day she told me she wished me dead. Dealing with my anger for her is an on-going struggle, but the fact

ALEX JONES

that she deems herself the victim and continues to hold me responsible for the abuse and then for speaking out, helps me live with my inability to let go of my unhealthy anger for her, while preserving what I call healthy anger. Anger that won't allow her to hurt me.

At times, my anger for her flares up when I realize I didn't have parents, and I don't have parents today. Instead of having two people I could turn to for help, guidance and a safe haven, I have had to spend my entire life fighting them off.

I become angry when I am reminded of the fact that it was my mother's duty to remove our boogeyman from us, and not mine. I confided in her, and she turned against me. I stood in a dock in a court, explaining myself to strangers. I stood alone.

I thought I needed reassurance from her, that I did the right thing. I thought I needed to understand why she hated me so intensely. I thought it was my burden to change so that she could love me. I thought I was unlovable. I thought I had to prove myself to her. I thought I owed the rest of my life to her. I thought I was her boogeyman, and my father's monster.

I thought all these things because she never told me anything differently, and because of that, my anger for her stays. It gives me the power I had once lost over my life. It helps me

ALEX JONES

maintain boundaries and allows me the choice to live my life without them.

It gives me a sense of freedom from her anger. It makes me feel larger than her, so as to defeat the emotional turmoil she once flung me into. My anger for her has given me back my power, my me'ness, my will to survive, my dreams, my hopes and my ability to function normally.

My anger for them both has given me the tools to run in the opposite direction when raising my children. It has provided me with the ability to love, nurture, care for and protect them from anything remotely harmful. It has opened my eyes to a world without monsters and boogeyman. It has encouraged me to be better and do better. My anger for her and the world I was caged in, has turned me into the person I once needed.

My anger for my father is different. It's limited and it stays behind in a world without The Afterwards. I am angry that he introduced me to my boogeyman, and then turning my world upside down after. I am angry that he hurt me and forced me to keep our secret.

I am angry that he beat my mother, my brother, sisters and I. I am angry that he abused alcohol and turned into a drunk.

ALEX JONES

## THE AFTERWARDS
### BROKEN DAUGHTERS: MADE BY BROKEN FATHERS

I am angry that he betrayed our religion and Church. I am angry that he blemished his image and ruined his reputation.

I am angry that he became stupid. I am angry that he brought the monsters with him. I am angry that he did this, day after day, night after night, for many years.

I am angry that I had to lay awake at night and watch the handle of my bedroom door. I am angry that there were times I couldn't breathe and was overcome with fear for him. I am angry that he hurt my sisters in the same way. I am angry that my Lily has to fight off her seizures on a daily basis and that it cripples her, because of him.

I am angry because there will never be family Christmas gatherings, Easter visits, birthday celebrations, or births to celebrate together. I am angry because we have all gone our separate ways and have created our own worlds to live in without each other.

But, as angry as I was with my father, I have forgiven him. My anger for him was lost in the early days of The Afterwards. I still believe that turning him in, was what expelled the boogeyman from him. I remember him for who he was before the day that it all changed. I loved him. I thought he was my hero. I remember him putting me to bed and kissing me on my

ALEX JONES

THE AFTERWARDS
BROKEN DAUGHTERS: MADE BY BROKEN FATHERS

forehead. Even though he thought I was asleep, I would hear him whisper he loves me. I remember him waking me up just before 9pm on a Saturday night, to watch a movie he thought I'd enjoy. I remember him ordering me an entire music collection from one of my favorite artists.

I remember him calling out to me on a sunny Saturday morning, loading me in his van, and picking my friends up one by one for an impromptu garden party in my honor. I remember him seeing me on the passage floor peeking over at the television when I though no-one could see, desperate to catch a glimpse of a series I wasn't allowed to watch. He never said a word.

I remember him buying me gifts each time I was struck down by an illness, or soft toys when I was hospitalized. I remember a time that he defended me, and that I felt loved by him. I blame the monsters and his own inner demons for stealing my father and replacing him with the boogeyman. Still, even though I have forgiven him, my bitterness and sadness shows up from time to time. It keeps me safe, and it grounds my decisions to remove myself from their lives.

For all that I had gone through to save my sisters from his clutches, it is a decision I would make over and over again. Given the same outcome, I would still walk into the lions' den for them.

ALEX JONES

BROKEN DAUGHTERS: MADE BY BROKEN FATHERS

But, what I can't do, is recover from the heartbreak my sisters plunged me into, leaving me with feelings of resentment towards them both.

They have allowed my mother to insert herself into their lives by convincing them that she was the real victim of my twisted self. I am angry at them for failing to stand by the truth of what my father had done, and for my mother's failure to protect us from him.

I am angry that they chose my mother's truth over mine and their own, over and over again. This, despite knowing what their own truth is. I am angry that they view me in the same light as my mother does and lay the same amount of blame on me.

Despite my anger for them, I am overcome with grief for losing them. With that in mind, I hold onto my anger for them, and hope that I can recover from the brokenness of losing them. More than anything, it helps me keep a safe distance between us so as to remain true to my truth. Anger helped me understand that my entire world is within me, and to find peace with all that's happened to me, I had to forgive myself my anger, and embrace it. So must you. Forgive your anger, especially if you've forgiven your abuser. Anger is power and it's a tool to protect yourself and your vulnerability. Get up each day, and show up to your life.

ALEX JONES

## THE AFTERWARDS
### BROKEN DAUGHTERS: MADE BY BROKEN FATHERS

Embrace the resentment that may show up from time to time, and instead of punishing yourself for it, use it to deal with your losses, and call it in to regain your power. Slow down to the things that damage you, and that that you were subjected to, and speed up to that which will revitalize your life again. Don't apologize for loving anyone, even if they didn't love you back, instead, learn to say no, and avoid anger for yourself.

Prioritize that which forms part of your healing and your plan for your life and break up with that which will evoke anger at yourself. Your imperfections are only yours, and only for you to judge, so love them. Stand your ground and stand tall each time you tell your truth. Don't surrender to theirs just to avoid an argument. It will eventually cause turmoil and ignite fury for yourself. The drama is no longer yours, and nobody but you know the true extent of your pain. Live for your joy. Forgive yourself the anger you feel towards those that have hurt you.

ALEX JONES

# KICK YOUR FEAR

I never wanted to expose my father or turn him in. I just couldn't live with the fear anymore. I was terrified of my bedroom at night, and when the door closed, I would lay awake at night watching and waiting for the handle on my door to turn.

I didn't want to fear sleep anymore, and I didn't want to be terrified of the monsters that would reach for me in the darkest hours of the night. I didn't want to hide under my bed, or in a closet praying that he wouldn't find me, even though I knew he would. I feared the smell of his breath, and his weight on top of me. I feared the pain of 'the thing,' and the monsters he would bring with him.

I was shown what I never wanted to see while plunged into a kind of fear I never thought I'd survive. Each meeting would leave me feeling sick and terrified of what would happen next. It was never really necessary to command me to lay still, I was already frozen with fear and my body was lifeless while overcome with horror and disbelief. I would lay there trembling into the

ALEX JONES

inner core of me. My heart would beat erratically, leaving me barely able to breathe.

The numbness that I would feel, and my inability to respond to my fear had turned into the one thing I would fear more than life itself. I would fear the sounds of his car as he pulled into our driveway, and at the same time, I feared the sound of my mother's car leaving. I feared the slamming of doors, and the sound whiskey makes when it's poured.

I feared that my father would carry out his threats of harming us, my mother and sisters. I was afraid that he might shoot us, one by one. I thought he might drive us into a brick wall, as he had done once or twice, before stopping inches away. I thought he would hurt my mother more severely. I thought he would kill her, and us.

I was terrified that my Lily was going to die. I thought that her little body couldn't handle the seizures for much longer. I was horrified seeing her convulse and recognizing the fear in her own eyes. I was terrified of telling my mother about our boogeyman, and then, afraid after she told on me. Yet, the fear I was living during the years of abuse, seemed nothing compared to the fear I was entrapped in, in The Afterwards. There was nothing to prepare me for the cruel way in which speaking out would come back to haunt me, when it flung me into a kind of fear, I was not yet acquainted with.

The terror was different, but the same. I had transitioned from the prey to the perpetrator almost overnight. The tables had turned, and the outcome I was desperate for, was nothing more than an unrealistic dream. In the end, I was the monster.

I began fearing every single little word I would ever say and every action I would ever take. I feared the questions and the interrogations. I feared that everything I said out loud was being analyzed and dissected by people desperate to prove me a liar.

I feared telling my story in that I would miss a word, forget an event or remember another. I feared the blame, the accusations, the shame, and the anger everyone else was projecting on me. I feared the distance that was created between me, and everyone else. Like a plague that was about to infest their lives, I was kept at a distance as though I would rub off on them.

The Afterwards had swooped in, removing me from the horrors of 'the thing,' only to place me into a new kind of terror. In my solitude, it brought new nightmares, and brand-new thoughts. It took me back to the torments of 'the thing' that

THE AFTERWARDS
BROKEN DAUGHTERS: MADE BY BROKEN FATHERS

wasn't quite ready to release me. I was overcome with fear that we, not one of us, were going to survive.

I couldn't see a future for any of us, and it scared me almost to death. In The Afterwards, the darkness crept up on me, and I could do nothing more than just exist. I went into each morning and each evening as a no-one, a nothing. I feared what I had done, and I feared the consequences. I feared my mother's wrath and hatred, which in turn, left me fearing my loneliness, abandonment and isolation. I was no longer a part of anything. When the others looked at me, I couldn't deny the shame and disgust in their eyes. I was mortified and revolted by my role in 'the thing,' and my life in The Afterwards.

I spent the first few years of my life fearing the boogeyman, and then I spent the next few fearing The Afterwards. It was again a kind of fear I couldn't deal with and a kind of fear, I hope to never know again. It was the only kind of fear that had the ability to paralyze me and keep me frozen by both my mother and my father.

I spent much time punishing myself for the extensive and on-going fear I was experiencing both during the abuse, and The Afterwards. I felt like I was lacking a single brave hair on my body, and that my courage had failed me when I needed it the most.

ALEX JONES

## THE AFTERWARDS
### BROKEN DAUGHTERS: MADE BY BROKEN FATHERS

But, much later in life, I realized that speaking out, despite the crippling fear that was opposing my decisions, was extraordinarily brave. I didn't deserve a life of fear, nor does any other child. My father used it during 'the thing' to control me, and exert power over me and then, my mother used it in The Afterwards to instill feelings of shame, guilt and self-hatred in me.

The thing about courage is, despite your fear, you are brave anyways. Living with and through fear is not a weakness. Facing our days and nights in fear, doesn't mean we are cowards. It means we are stronger than we ever thought we were. Looking into the eyes of our boogeymen and monsters, is terrifying and debilitating, but we did it.

Our fear was never a shame. The fear instilled in us was used to control our silence. Forgive yourself your fear. You were right to be afraid. You had every reason to be terrified. The horrors you lived through was frightening. You did it, despite your fear.

Fear will always be a part of you and your story. Some days, because of your fear, you will move mountains, and other days, you will surrender to it. There will be times that you will tell stories around your fear, but then there will be moments that

ALEX JONES

your story silences you with fear. You don't have to mask it, or explain it. You are safe now. You are supported in your fear. With each obstacle you climb in the name of overcoming your fear, you are stronger.

You are worthy, you always have been. You no longer have to feel so small, your fear has made you a giant. You have crossed oceans and climbed mountains, even though you were afraid. Your fear has crippled and isolated you. Forgive yourself your fear. You were never supposed to be scared into fearing your abuser, your life, your voice and your survival.

Your sadness is a direct result of the fact that you were wronged, thereby losing something that you may never get back. Avoiding the sadness phase, will only prolong it when you at last, surrender to it.

This is a time when your you'ness becomes extraordinarily sensitive and makes you vulnerable to intense heartache and emotional pain. Even though it is temporary and does pass, it is one of the most excruciating phases I've had to deal with. I thought that hiding my sorrow from the world, would make me untouchable but, all it did was keep the emotions bouncing around inside of me. You don't have to hold back your tears to show strength. Denying yourself your sadness will only immerse you deeper into a kind of darkness you are fighting tooth and nail to get out of.

We all move through the different stages of The Afterwards at different rates. Sometimes, we might feel we are so close to normal again, but at other times, we can bounce around between the stages we are flung into. There are moments you will find yourself in disbelief and shock again, still unsure of how it all happened and how you got to where you are now. You might reach a stage that leaves you debilitated and crippled again, as it mercifully numbs you to the intense heartache that threatens to absorb your entire being. Phases are delayed, and some are rushed, but the one thing I can promise you, they are equally harsh. Bouts of anger, resignation, resentment, sleeplessness, bitterness, and repeated lingering in the abuse might overwhelm you when you least expect it. Finally, through it all and at a time you might never see coming, you will find acceptance.

You don't have to be brave all the time. Moments of happiness will slowly reappear in your life, and sadness will no longer affect you as profoundly as it once did.

ALEX JONES

# THE AFTERWARDS
## BROKEN DAUGHTERS: MADE BY BROKEN FATHERS

**ALEX JONES**

# DROPS OF SHAME, BUCKETS OF GUILT

Once the shock of the backlash of my turning my father in started wearing off, I was overcome by guilt for bringing disgrace into our family's lives. It left me feeling like I was responsible for a new label in which we would be identified as garbage. Trash. Low-class or second-hand humans. As though that wasn't enough of a cross to bear, the guilt I was immediately submerged in for being the reason my mother and sisters were broken, flung me into a dark hole where I felt powerless, unable to move and devastated.

I blamed myself for hurting my mother and making her a casualty of my war. The guilt I felt was all consuming and defeating. I knew what it felt like when I discovered the truth about my sisters, so I watched my mother, and prayed that if she had ever discovered the truth, she would forgive herself. She didn't know then. I watched her when she thought I wasn't looking, and I prayed that she would never punish herself for something she had no control over, and never knew of. Like a

ALEX JONES

hawk, my eyes were constantly on her as I tried to identify her emotions and her state of mind. Once she had read my letter, there were still no signs of responsibility, and it scared me to think that I was having an enormously hard time trying to forgive myself for what was happening to my sisters, yet, my mother had no trouble with it at all. At once, she was the victim. The only victim.

I felt immensely guilty for failing my sisters, and as much as I never wanted my mother to feel responsible for our boogeyman's indiscretions, her inability to feel anything at all entirely unnerved me.

The guilt found a home inside of me for years after the abuse. As much as I tried to make sense of where I went wrong, how I didn't see my sisters' abuse, and what I could have done to handle the outcome better, the guilt continued to haunt me while the shame continued to taunt me.

I tried to find something else each day to blame myself for, and each time I tried to identify my role in the abuse. Did I lead him on? Was it something I said? Was it something I wore? Was it the way I looked at him?

My guilt was similar to a deadly virus that was eating away at me at a rapid speed. Not only the immense guilt for

# THE AFTERWARDS
## BROKEN DAUGHTERS: MADE BY BROKEN FATHERS

turning him in, alienating my mother, sisters, and brother from all that they loved, not only for the blackness my mother found herself in, in The Afterwards, but also for not protecting my sisters.

I watched my mother deal with her emotions. I watched her come to terms with losing her husband, her home, and all she had accumulated in the years of her marriage to him. I never wanted that for her, and I never blamed her for the dysfunction in our home. Then. I saw her as much a victim as I was. I feared for her, but never feared her. Then.

I was convinced that for the remainder of my life, I would be overshadowed and drown in the shame that I thought would impenetrably follow me from the moment I found my voice. It was as though I was hearing an angry me tell myself that as I continuously tried to find my place in society, amongst others and with my own family, I never could. I had no place. I didn't matter. I changed the course of all our lives when I made the decision to rescue my sisters and I from the clutches of a monster I had learned to fear. I made the decision. Me. Angry me told myself that I was selfish. Inconsiderate. Self-serving.

It was only when I told my sisters that there was nothing in the world that they could have done to initiate the abuse, that

ALEX JONES

## THE AFTERWARDS
### BROKEN DAUGHTERS: MADE BY BROKEN FATHERS

I forgave myself a little more. It was only then that I began to imagine a possibility that I had no choice in what happened to us. I so often wish my mom had told me that it was never my fault, many years before.

I thought I had to find absolution for what I had done when I turned my father in. I was living in a world I had no experience in, and one where I was living the guilt I was feeling. My thoughts, my prayers, my breaths and the way I looked at the world, was compromised by the guilt that had become me. I was afraid to think, knowing that my thoughts were nothing more than a danger to me, and to the people around me. Punishing myself was easy, but I could never find the punishment that I felt was suitable for the crime I had committed.

I wanted to understand why my father hurt us. I wanted to understand how it was possible that a monster had taken up residence in his body. I was desperate to pinpoint the moment it all went wrong, and it all changed. I thought that if I could figure it all out, and if I could make sense of the trauma, we had all found ourselves in, I could fix it for us all. I wanted to apologize; I just never knew what for. I wanted to put things back to the way they were, but I couldn't. I couldn't for one reason only, I could never hand my sisters over to my father again. It was never my job to understand what had happened to us. It was never on my

ALEX JONES

shoulders to justify what my father had done, or why he had turned into our worst nightmare. It was never my place to apologize for seeking help and liberation from the devil wearing my father, and ultimately, the mother who was tasked with protecting us. It was never my fault.

It will never be your fault. Your monster was real, and as much as you try to hide or deny it, it doesn't deserve presence in your life, or from the mouth of someone else. It might control you in the early days after you speak out, but there is nothing shameful that you are responsible for. The emotions and rollercoaster rides you go on, is controlled through your guilt which once again, gives your monster the power you worked so hard to take back. It's not your fault. It's not because you wore a revealing dress, a low-cut top, or short skirts. You weren't abused because you were affectionate with your abuser, or because his love for you was tainted.

He didn't betray or violate you because you looked at him inappropriately or smiled at him "enticingly." A child knows nothing of inappropriate gazes or enticing smiles. A child knows no perversion or much about allure or appeal.

The mere discussion of the shame that was brought into our lives, was in itself a shameful topic of discussion. It had the

ALEX JONES

power to bring out the control it had over my life. The abuser will never own up to the shameful abuse, and it leaves us with the burden to carry it and once again, imprisons us in a cage for something we never had control over.

Realistically speaking, it is important to understand that your abuser was the one with power. It was his choice to exact power over you when yours were limited. The shame I felt for the abuse left me with a certainty that there was something wrong with me. I began isolating myself from the world around me, and even though I was plunged into a frightening loneliness, I felt safer trapped in my own shame, guilt and grief than I did having to face up to it.

I wanted to become perfect so that my imperfections were never again exposed to the world. I strived for a life where my thoughts, words and actions were perfect in the desperate hope that people would forget the shameful thing that happened to our family. Making mistakes brought out a kind of rage in me for myself, I never thought I could feel. I had to be better. I had to do better. I wasn't the abused child any longer, and I wanted the world to forget that it ever happened. I wanted to forget it ever happened. But, breaking the silence of the secrets I was so desperate to veil was what ultimately freed me from myself, my father and my shame. Identify the fact that you were never to

# THE AFTERWARDS
## BROKEN DAUGHTERS: MADE BY BROKEN FATHERS

blame for the abuse. It is your abuser's cross to bear. He betrayed you, and the people closest to him. My father was the head of our home, the leader of our pack, and the maker of our tribe who destroyed all that once was good.

When someone tells you that you were right to speak up, believe them. When you are commended for having a voice, know that you deserved commendation. Applaud yourself for suffering through the bravest thing you have ever done, and probably ever will do.

These are the tools you will need to raise your voice when you must. Surround yourself with those who make you feel safe to speak out, and who will provide you with the know-how to forgive yourself afterwards.

You have lost just as much as any other member of your family did, and as much as it never was their fault, it wasn't yours either. It wasn't then, and it never will become your burden to live with. I had so many words I couldn't say, so much turmoil I needed my mother to know about, but my voice sickened her. The sight of me repulsed her, and the way my facial expressions angered her kept me moving around undetected, and under the radar. The Afterwards never ends, and never goes away. Your life is The Afterwards because nothing comes after. But, how you

ALEX JONES

## THE AFTERWARDS
### BROKEN DAUGHTERS: MADE BY BROKEN FATHERS

treat yourself after the abuse will define your life moving forwards. In the immediate moments of The Afterwards, how you see yourself and what you think of yourself, will live in your space for years to come.

Most of what matters the most will happen after the abuse ends. Each moment that forced me to question every single event, happened afterwards. The guilt came afterwards. The shame came afterwards. The disillusionment came afterwards. The sadness came afterwards. Despite all the challenges that lurks after the abuse, there are still not enough reasons to remain silent, and endure ongoing sexual abuse. I was painfully aware of the part I played in The Afterwards. I never excused my responsibility in putting us there, and I never tried to minimize my actions even though it was not my job to save my sisters or myself. I noticed the stares and I heard the faint utterings all around me, but I never said much to defend myself or my actions. Instead, I believed what everyone else was saying about me, about what I had done, and I punished myself for it all. The distance between me, my mother and sisters grew, but when I crossed over into their space, their silence conquered me.

But, just like me, you will reach a moment in time when your voice will become louder against those who attack your honesty, and place shame on your past as you continue on your journey to your new normal. I can't tell you this enough, it was never your shame to bear. You were a child and could in no way at all, stand up to a man who was not only someone of authority, but someone you probably trusted. What happened was shameful, but it was not your shame. Hands down, the monster was the master of the shame we thought were ours.

# THE AFTERWARDS
## BROKEN DAUGHTERS: MADE BY BROKEN FATHERS

ALEX JONES

# CHOOSE YOU

While living in 'the thing,' I found myself at war with the fact that I was being forced to function normally and live in a life that had treated me unkindly. I felt unwanted in a world that had only shown suffering to me. I couldn't understand why I needed to be alive when as a child, and later as a teenager, I knew only of cruelty.

I thought I wasn't strong or brave enough. Living with 'the thing' and then being catapulted into The Afterwards brought out my intense desire to find a way out of this world. I wanted a way out of a life I hated. I wanted to feel something other than heartache and suffocation. I no longer wanted to decipher my emotions or identify the triggers. I was exhausted. I was tired of walking on eggshells around everyone. I was emotionally spent by having to consider each word and every action.

A way out seemed like an only option. I couldn't stop thinking about it, and I thought it might be the answer to my

ALEX JONES

prayers. I wanted a break from it all. I just wanted out. The more I thought about it, the happier I became. I approached, what I thought would be my last days, with enthusiasm. The idea of having control over my pain, lifted my mood considerably. For the first time in an entire lifetime, I was excited about something in my life, even though it would lead to the end of it.

There was a promise in it that the fear, shame, guilt and heartache would be over soon, and that my heart could finally stop beating a mile a minute each time my bedroom door opened, or my mother's voice was raised. The idea that my stomach would no longer hurt or cripple me, and the constricting lump in my throat would never show up again, was something I was eager to cast aside. The very thought of never having to face my parents again, left me feeling as though I could breathe without effort.

I wanted to control something again. I wanted to take charge of my life, and my me'ness again. As I began planning every detail of my ending, I was rudely interrupted by unexpected doubts that began nagging at me. My sisters would be alone, and my mother couldn't be trusted with their well-being. I was horrified to realize that my boogeyman would replace me with my sisters. Whether or not they knew it or would ever admit to it, they wanted me to live, and they needed me to live. My mother had checked out of the reality of 'the thing,' and I knew that my sisters would never survive in my place and face the monsters as I did. My father's brutality and aggression had escalated drastically and had reached a point where I thought each day would be our last. I had no way of knowing what the endgame would be. I wanted to protect them. I was all they had. I began looking around me and noticed how wonderful life was for others. It was something that I was sure, was normal. A normal I hoped my sisters could find too, but for that to happen, I had to stay. I had to live.

What I didn't realize at the time was that the fight in me, wanted me in this world, and not only for others, but for my own survival. Suddenly, I had a new goal. I had hope. I wanted to overcome all that was trying to get me to leave.

Each night I thought I could never live through, I did. Despite doubting whether I was present for my sisters, I was. Even though I was determined to discard all that I thought I couldn't do even for one more day, I began crossing back and forth between a thin line of wanting to be free and wanting to help my sisters survive.

I wanted to give my sisters and I the best shot at surviving, and without realizing it, I wanted to survive for me. I wanted to make something wonderful out of our nothing. I wanted to repair instead of repeating. I wanted to swap our monsters for angels. I wanted to see my war through to the end and defeat it. I wanted to fight until it was alright to stop.

I wanted to live because I never wanted my monster, and later, my mother to defeat me. I wanted to be an example to my sisters, and I wanted them to look back and know that I did not fail them, and that I could never leave them. I wanted to prove to my mother that I was stronger than her hatred, accusations and desperate need to weaken me. I wanted to show my father, my boogeyman, that I could survive him.

Taking back your power, will leave you so much more powerful than your abuser ever was. Your determination and will to survive will turn you into someone so powerful, you'll forever be the someone that conquered the boogeyman.

There are a whole batch of stars out there, just waiting for you to reach up and climb on everyone. You are in the unique position where a reset command has taken place in your life, and now, you can paint your future and tailor-make it any which way you like.

But, for that to happen, you need life. You must live. You must put one foot in front of the other, one minute at a time.

ALEX JONES

## THE AFTERWARDS
### BROKEN DAUGHTERS: MADE BY BROKEN FATHERS

These steps will turn into days, weeks, months and years. Your voice will become louder each day you choose to survive, making it hard for your monster to exact power or control over you.

Your name is worth so much more than a label you place on yourself. You are more than an abused daughter. Instead of whispering your name, say it out loud and in pride because, you never gave up. You never surrendered. You chose life. You never left the battlefield.

You never stopped to fight for your you'ness. You conquered your demons and that of your monster because you were always, always, stronger than he was.

Your scars will fade when you choose you. Most people who learn of my life as an abused daughter say they can't find my scars, and had I not spoken about my ordeal, they would never have known. I tell them it's because they no longer exist. There is nothing in my life that could give away the fact that I had lived my entire childhood at the hands of a monster.

There is nothing of evidence to prove that I broke beyond repair, and there are no shards visible to the eye that have had to be glued back together. I chose life, despite my mother's absence. I was my own warrior, and stood up to return and integrated back into a society I wanted to function normally in.

ALEX JONES

## THE AFTERWARDS
### BROKEN DAUGHTERS: MADE BY BROKEN FATHERS

I chose life because I wanted to succeed. I wanted to achieve what I once thought was impossible, the impossible life handed me, and the one my broken mother thought I'd fail in.

I will live the remainder of my life knowing that I had risen up with courage in my heart, and a smile on my face, despite my mother's rejection of me. I chose me.

You are a survivor. You might have spent your entire life trying to become someone the world, and more importantly, your abuser would approve of. It hasn't taken the pain away, and it hasn't made you feel loved. It's time to approve of yourself, despite what others don't see or understand. Let the world see your strength, especially when you want to hide, so no-one sees your pain. If I can tell you one more thing, it's to never listen to the opinion of someone judging you on how you are dealing with your pain, when they have never been called to fight a war of boogeymen and monsters, like you have.

ALEX JONES

# YOUR MONSTER, YOUR DEVIL

"Your war is not so much against the abuse, but rather, the darkness you find yourself in, and the participants of your exploitation."

I remember as a little girl, my mind had a way of manifesting an image of what evil should look like. When I heard about demons, satan, evil, monsters and boogeyman, I pictured a grotesque being so horrendous, my mind could barely identify what I was seeing. An image of an enormous red man-animal with horns, black and red eyes, and a tail that would stand over me, and frighten me almost to death. I imagined his teeth so big, sharp and protruding, it could bite off an entire arm or leg, while he carries a fork that was dipped in fire only moments before.

But, as I grew up, and after meeting my own boogeyman, I began realizing that monsters, devils and demons were much better equipped to function and live amongst us by attacking a human body and taking on their form. When it took my father, I was horrified to discover that it could take anybody. It was a

ALEX JONES

# THE AFTERWARDS
## BROKEN DAUGHTERS: MADE BY BROKEN FATHERS

terrible shock to my system to realize that my father, who was the holiest of us all, the mightiest of the world, and the smartest of man by far, was penetrated, removed and replaced by a monster. It came for him, and it defeated him. He didn't stand a chance against that which stole his body. The devil was wearing my father.

To admit to myself that my father was gone, and that a monster had taken up residence inside of him, was something I could never bring myself to say out loud. I didn't want others to know, and more than anything, I tried to shield my sisters and my mother from the monster pretending to be our father. All I knew for sure was that this "thing" was sent by satan to not only infiltrate our lives, but to ruin it in the process.

Even though I couldn't see the monster's grotesqueness, I knew he was living in our home and posing as our father. That our lives were in danger from that moment on, was a feeling I couldn't ignore, or a fear I couldn't shake. For each moment he was around us, I was terrified that any one of those moments could be our last. He was a great pretender and a master manipulator who had completely fooled the world. Not only was my mother, sisters, brother, our Church, friends and family unable to see what I was seeing, but it was as though they were becoming increasingly bewitched by him. They couldn't see what

# THE AFTERWARDS
## BROKEN DAUGHTERS: MADE BY BROKEN FATHERS

I saw. They couldn't hear why I heard. It was only me. It was when I realized that no-one in the world would ever believe that the monster was real. Attending Church was becoming increasingly daunting for me. I could barely focus on the sermon as I sat watching him, wondering why God wasn't revealing him to the world.

I couldn't understand how the forces of evil were allowed passage into our Church. I listened when he spoke, and I recognized my father's voice. He spoke exactly like my father did. He limped slightly, just like my father did. He laughed out loud and beautifully, just like my father did. His skin was pale, his hands still bore evidence of his hard work, but it wasn't him.

I wanted to find proof of the monster inside of him in the things he said and did, and hope that somehow, he would slip up and reveal himself. Aside from the nightly visits, there never was anything I could put my finger on that I could use as proof that it was not him. I didn't understand the world he was from and had no inclination of how to fight him.

But, it wasn't always about monsters and boogeymen. There were times when I thought I could see my father again. Moments like those that I could hear his true voice. During those seconds, there was something gentler inside of him. It felt normal

ALEX JONES

for a while. I was hopeful and optimistically overjoyed for those glimpses, even though they were fleeting. Those moments were so short that I could never find a way to keep him with us and beg him to fight against the monster who kept returning. I had hoped each time that he would stay. I was excited that the terrifying nights might finally be over. In those moments, I felt safe again. I thought he'd won, but he never did. I thought he had fought against the devil that wore him and won.

I desperately fought against what I told myself, he wasn't. I was waging a war against what he had become, and who it was living inside of him. I was on a battlefield with a monster creating havoc inside of him, and I fought tooth and nail to bring my father back to us.

What I didn't realize in the early days was that at the same time as fighting for my father, I was fighting a warfare within myself. Along the way, I lost faith that he would come back permanently, leaving me to be on guard each moment of every single day. I grew increasingly despondent and angry that he couldn't muster up enough strength to fight harder against his demons. The man, my father and hero, was nothing at all. He was weak. He was defeated. He was conquered by a darkness, and our love for him could not save him. I was devastated by the fact that he couldn't love us enough, to fight for us. He betrayed me.

ALEX JONES

# THE AFTERWARDS
## BROKEN DAUGHTERS: MADE BY BROKEN FATHERS

He betrayed my sisters. He betrayed us all. I didn't want him telling me what to do, or what was right or wrong anymore. I didn't believe he knew, and I hated the fact that he was allowed to discipline and teach us. He was the bad man we were warned about. He was the stranger we were taught not to speak to or accept a ride from. He was the man a court would label as evil. He was not my father. I no longer trusted him and questioned everything he said. Still, he was invincible and untouchable to the rest of the world. It was only me that knew, and I was determined to keep him from tainting what I knew was wrong and right.

As a child, I was unable to separate myself from him since I had very little power over my own life. Just like most children, I was taught about evil, satan, great pretenders and liars, yet I could never identify to the world that my father was that.

Just like I was, you were probably threatened with the consequences of speaking out. You might have wanted to protect a mother, a sibling, or another member of your family. Once your abuser convinces you that speaking out will harm someone you love, they have taken the first step to exert control over you and establish the power they are desperate to own.

As a result of my fear for other family members, I was desperate to keep our secret and find other ways to cope. My

ALEX JONES

body remained behind during the abuse, but my mind took me to a place that kept me alive night after night.

I had no doubt that monsters, demons and boogeyman are active in our world, and were functioning in our home. I knew too that our little bit of evil moved around freely, and undetected to the rest of the world.

Your abuser is a great pretender and liar. His charm and deceptions gave him an appeal and charisma that drew others to him. He probably was an impressive influencer, and as time went on, and as he asserted himself into your community, his power, charm and deceptions made a respected man out of him.

He won't abide by any rules, and your battles with him were never fair. His authority over you, was what left you vulnerable and weakened you. You had no chance.

Whatever he inflicts upon you, it is more than likely you interpreted it as punishment for something you must have done wrong. I spent so much time analyzing my behavior, the way I dressed, the way I walked, the way I spoke, and the way I looked in a desperate attempt to ward off the attacks. As a result of this, I spent many years being hyper vigilant of my behavior, and who I was. It stole so much peace from me in the early years. What someone should have told me was that I was an innocent in the depraved mind of a monster, and it's something I am telling you now.

There is never a reason for your abuser to have abused you. There never was anything in your behavior or appearance to warrant his depravity. You were not being punished, and you did nothing to merit or justify the abuse.

Your abuser had a distorted rationality of logic he used to indoctrinate you. By isolating you, threatening you, degrading you, and then, indulging you, he has managed to gain power and control over you. By demanding that you keep his actions a "secret," he began isolating you from someone you might have taken into your confidence when the abuse began. With each abusive event, his control over you strengthened, and as a result, your isolation increased.

The same can be said by threatening you. It is imperative that he cultivates fear and hopelessness in an effort to keep you under his control so that you couldn't resist the abuse or speak out about it. More often than not, your abuser threatened harm to a loved one, or threatened to harm himself which left you feeling responsible for his well-being.

Degrading me was one of the most effective tools both my mother and father used to strip me of any power I had left.

ALEX JONES

## THE AFTERWARDS
### BROKEN DAUGHTERS: MADE BY BROKEN FATHERS

Shortly after the abuse began, and when The Afterwards came around, my self-esteem was almost beyond repair. My mother would regularly tell me how ugly I was, how black and hard my heart was, how impossible I was to love, and how nobody could stand the sight of me. She would remind me as often as she could that I was responsible for the abuse, and that I "enticed" my father.

My father would persistently remind me that he was the only man that could love me, and that nobody could love someone like me, the way he did. Even though I excelled at school, I felt stupid. Not smart enough. Not pretty enough. Not friendly enough. When I started isolating myself from friends and family, a new label was placed on me by my friends; they thought I thought I was better than anyone else. In an attempt to hide not only from the world and the possibility that the abuse could be discovered, but I was also seen as a snob. When I felt I could no longer bear the abuse, or the harsh words from my mother, my father would somehow sense my desperation, and indulge me. He would allow me short periods of freedom, he normally never would. He would buy me expensive gifts and treat me to lunch or a movie. He would bring me music from my favorite singer and rent a movie he knew I would love. It was during those moments

ALEX JONES

that he hit a reset button on my almost falling apart and exposing him for the monster he was.

It was during those episodes that I would feel guilty for seeing him as a boogeyman and excuse his behavior as a side-effect of his drinking. It was during those days that I would find hope again and believe in the possibility of a life without the abuse.

The truth is, moments like those were transitory, and forgotten almost as soon as they were over. His methods to manipulate me was formed around my personality, and my desperation to be normal.

What I didn't realize at the time was that my days of indulgences were just another tactic to enforce fear, defenselessness and enslavement. His behavior was unpredictable and caused immense panic and stress in not only my life, but in the lives of us all.

Through sheer desperation, I did all I could to alter my mindset to that of being the perpetrator. I hated myself, and I hated the chaos I had brought into all our lives. I wanted more than anything to feel better about myself, and fight for a life I so desperately wanted to carve out for myself. I stood up to my mother, determined not to surrender to her cruel and harsh words. I was adamant to rise above her cruelty, and not allow her to have the same, crushing power over me as my father once did.

But the moment I confronted my mother during one of our many arguments, I felt horrible. I was devastated by the fact that I wanted to hurt my mother. I wanted her to feel what I had felt when she hurt me, yet I felt worse trying to do to her what she did to me.

Using my words and anger to destroy her emotionally, just made me feel like I was someone else. Perhaps a monster in her eyes. I was rudely awakened to the fact that I was giving her a reason to hate me. I never felt any better after spewing harsh words at her, instead, I was confirming all she had said about me. I was ugly. My heart was hard and black. I was trouble. I was an awful person.

My anger towards her was showing her everything I wasn't. It was stealing my me'ness from me and turning me into her. I wasn't my mother, and I never wanted to be anything like she was. Violence was her way to settle disputes and resolve differences. It was what she knew. It was what my father taught her. It was how he treated her, and us. It wasn't me. It wasn't what I was going to take away from the years of abuse. I began realizing what was best for me, and while I started listening to what I was feeling, my mother's anger increased, her manipulation intensified, her lies and deceit became merciless. The closer I moved into a direction I wanted to take, the more heartless she became. It was almost as though she sensed that I was no longer her emotional sounding board. I reluctantly made peace with her anger towards me, and I kept reminding myself that I was not lost. I was just different.

The closer I got to victory, the more my mother would blame and shame me. But, just like my father, she was a master manipulator who was able to keep her anger and hatred of me supressed from the rest of the world. I will never forget the day she heard of a situation where another daughter was abused, and how she was the first to condemn her parents. When my mother immediately accused the girl's mother of being unable to protect her daughter, I was flabbergasted. I was stunned, and shocked by her carelessness.

With that in mind, I was more determined than ever to succeed in The Afterwards, even though her abhorrence of me had increased drastically. It had finally reached a point where an explosion between us took place, one where she confessed to her intense revulsion of me, and how she hoped I would die. As much as it devastated me to hear her say it, and as much as it derailed me each time she would carelessly make it clear that I was nothing to her, that I had no meaning in her life, and that my death would bring her endless joy, I continued on with my fight for my wonderful, afraid that if I didn't, my fight would turn into my very own inner demons, and I would become a monster to someone else.

If only I knew then that her admission to what I had always known, brought me the closure I never knew I needed, I would have thanked her for her truth, even though it hurt. For the first time in all my years under my mother's razor sharp tongue, did I find relief, and I could breathe freely. The hurt I was feeling was somewhat engulfing, but the fact that it was never a figment of my imagination, or an idealism I had dreamed up regarding her detestation and inability to connect with me, was liberating.

I finally heard her say what I always knew to be true. I no longer lingered between uncertainty and clarity. It was never my mind that was broken or fractured. It was never an excuse to gain sympathy or attention. She did not love me. She could not love me, and she was quite fine about it.

For your journey, you will be flung into so many emotions when your abuser is unable to take responsibility for what he has done to you. It is important to understand that when they lose a confrontation, they almost always claim to not be in control of themselves or the abuse inflicted upon you.

From making excuses, to blaming and redefining the harmful acts towards you by implying that the problem was never with them, but with you or the outside world, they seek to maintain control over you. Your monster was real. Your boogeyman lived in your space, and almost entirely consumed you. Never apologize for what he has done to you, and never try and find the reason for his behaviour in your actions, or inside of you somewhere. It was calculated on his behalf and carried out while knowing what he was doing.

Even if you stand alone, stand up for yourself and stand firm against your abuser. Your truth will always be yours. Own it and use it. Find your wonderful. Call back the person you were before the abuse and build on that. Grow on who you were before they tried to destroy you.

The best revenge is your success. Claim it. Be it. Live it.

**ALEX JONES**

# THE AFTERWARDS
## BROKEN DAUGHTERS: MADE BY BROKEN FATHERS

**ALEX JONES**

# FIND YOUR TRIBE VIBES

For a while, and immediately after you've spoken out against your abuser, you might find yourself right in the center of a whole lot of nothingness. Nothing to look forward to. Nothing and no-one around to comfort you. Nothing to remove a whole new way to fear the past and dread the future. Nothing or no-one to promise you that you will be okay, and that tomorrow is a chance for a better life. Nothing and no-one to tell you that you did the right thing, and that you courageously fought a battle many others will never be called to.

From the moment I walked away from my mother, my sisters and my past, I was trampled by sudden and unanticipated encounters. People were coming into my life, and changing my view on the world, and the people who inhabit it. My entire existence was altered, and I began seeing myself through the eyes of others.

Through my experiences with people who were nothing more than strangers at first, I realized the full extent of my

ALEX JONES

## THE AFTERWARDS
### BROKEN DAUGHTERS: MADE BY BROKEN FATHERS

world's brokenness. Some people I would meet would say that I was beautiful. Others would complement me on speaking well. Some would say that I have a kind heart, and that I am a really great listener. Out of the blue, someone would say that I was easy to talk to, and that my reaction to other's problems was true and heartfelt. Someone else would say that I was a good person, that I had an amazing heart, and a great personality.

Over the years, I began believing these people I began connecting with as my journey took another turn. Total strangers would show up, stay, and never leave or give up on me. Even though it brought me to a place where I began believing things people were saying about me, I was saddened each time I would reflect on my mother's harsh and unkind words. As much as I tried, I still can't quite figure out why it was so important to my mother, to break me. Her unfiltered verbal beatings, was something I could never inflict on anyone else, let alone my own daughter. I couldn't understand it.

These people became the family I was learning to live without in my life. Their presence, and the knowing that I mattered improved my quality of life immensely. I didn't have to find reasons to trust them. I didn't have to wait for a monster to appear, or anger lurking around inside of them. I didn't have to question their every word, and more than all that was important

# THE AFTERWARDS
## BROKEN DAUGHTERS: MADE BY BROKEN FATHERS

in my life, I never questioned their loyalty. As a result, my faith was restored in a world that almost defeated me. I trusted other humans again, and because of that, I learned to trust the world again. These were the people I could, feel and who made sense to my crooked life.

What I initially thought was fleeting, taught me that people do stay. They showed me a side that I had never seen before. They were like a pack of wolves who showed up not just on the first day, but each day after. As my life settled into a normal kind of life, these were the people who accepted me despite a questionable past. This was my tribe; one I could choose and make a family out of. It was who brought me out from my nothingness and showed me that my footprints were important to this world.

My initial reaction to these meetings, was to run. I didn't want people so close to me again. I didn't want others to know who I was, or where I came from. I didn't want them to discover my secrets, and how ugly, black and hard-hearted I was. I didn't want to lose again. But, they taught me that my voice was as valuable as my mother's and my father's. They instilled a kind of calm and peace I needed, and they absolved me from my past. Almost as though The Afterwards was readjusting the stars, and uncrossing the wires, these wolves were as though they were appointed angels in my life. I was no longer listening to those I shared biology with. I stopped believing that they were dealt a severe blow by my speaking out against my father. I didn't have to listen to the cruel way in which I was being held responsible for The Afterwards. Instead, my tribe surrounded me, and showed me the truth of the hell I had been living in for most of my life.

The Afterwards wasn't all I thought it would be when I stepped in, in the early days. It wasn't all about destruction, hurt, anger, humiliation, blame, shame and guilt. The Afterwards wasn't only about hatred and vengeance. The Afterwards my tribe led me to was one of love, joy, peace, calm and family. It protected me, defended me, built me up, and kept me there each time I thought I'd fall. It lifted me higher each time I was sure I would fail. The Afterwards this tribe created for me, was one where I grew, overcame, conquered and finally found a purpose for my existence, despite my secrets. Despite my shame.

I no longer pretend that "the thing" never happened, and since The Afterwards began, I can recall many, many tribe vibes that have crossed paths with me at a time that I desperately needed them to. I didn't see it then. My distrust for people stopped me from recognizing the good they were bringing with them, but as I look back, I realize how lost I would still have been, had they never stepped into my life, and loved me for who I was, despite who I was related to. Some of these tribe vibes have faded into the background and into my new past while others have stayed and will remain extraordinarily present in my new Afterwards. With each one of them, and with each moment spent together, I became a little better. I grew a little more. I loved myself a little more each day, and I discarded the idea that I was shameful. My past was. What my father did was. Not me. Slowly, and without intending to, I became the person I once needed. I became what they saw in me.

Each one gave me a glimpse into a life I thought I could never have. With each one, I was given the opportunity to see myself as they did. A bond of sisters, a pack of wolves that fiercely preserved my heart, and untainted my stained spirit. They brought a lifeline with them and have kept it on hold for me ever since. Because of their presence, I have learned that the world is predominantly good. People can be trusted and loved. Monsters are real, but you and I have choices.

We don't owe our abusers or their followers an apology, or loyalty. We don't owe them restitution or devotion. We don't owe anybody an explanation or justification for what was done to us. You don't owe the world a damn thing. You owe it to only yourself to identify and embrace the fact that it happened to you.

ALEX JONES

## THE AFTERWARDS
### BROKEN DAUGHTERS: MADE BY BROKEN FATHERS

You didn't ask for it. You didn't initiate it. You couldn't have known anything about what you couldn't understand. You were a child. Only a child. Their child. Choosing a life without the demons from your past will help you let go of feelings of discomfort and guilt. It was never easy to make the decision to remove myself from my family. It wasn't any easier sticking to it, but keeping my distance from them was and is the only way I remain unaffected by them. Knowing that my mother's love for me could have altered The Afterwards and aid in our healing, makes me understand just how detached she was.

Distance from those that have hurt and abused you, those who brought about division and chaos into your life, and those who were supposed to fight beside you, is imperative for you to maintain, and not feel guilty about.

My mother was emotionally distressing to me, almost more intense than the abuse I suffered under my father. I loved and cared deeply for her. The loss I felt when she walked away from me each time she had sworn that she had changed, and that she wanted to do better, was devastating for a long while after she left.

It wasn't that we were no longer speaking the same language, we never did. It was time to let her go and cherish the

ALEX JONES

me'ness that I had found again. We were never on the same page, on the contrary, she was my greatest source of pain in The Afterwards. Her denunciations, the accusatory conversations between us, and finally, her inability to forgive my desperate need to survive was what ultimately removed her from my life. The tribe that was entering my life was unselfish and understood my inner battle. There was a time that I would have given up everything to have had the same connection with my mother and sisters. My tribe taught me much, almost as though they were standing in for what I was missing from not only my mother and father, but from my brother and sisters too.

What was meant to be an unconditional bond with her, turned into a conditional, self-serving and volatile union. I believed her when she told me that speaking out was wrong. I believed her when she told me I was ugly, hateful, spiteful, rebellious, artificial and that I was incapable of being loved. I believed her when she told me that I would never find someone who loved me, and that I was not deserving of anything that was good. It brought much chaos into my life and settled like dust onto my heart and into my spirit.

As mentioned in The Afterwards, what I didn't count on was the tribe vibes who would come in packs and encircle me. Because of their presence, I no longer saw myself through my mother's eyes. I began noticing fractions of myself through the eyes of these wolves. They stuck around, much longer than I thought they would, and they remained close. They re-taught me how to live again and they taught me to forgive myself. They showed me how to accept that what I did, was nothing more than my need to survive, and save my mother and sisters in the process.

As I slowly began waking up to their ideas, I realized that I felt less guilty and ashamed when there was enough distance between my mother and I. It was working for me. As much as it hurt my heart and tainted my spirit, it was working, and I was finding a reason to be present in this world again. For the first time in my life, I was able to identify and distinguish between the good and the not-so-good fractions that had come into my life.

I learned to filter out people that chose me based on what I could offer, making it impossible for me to value their presence. My mother would often show up and swear that she had changed, and that she loved me. She would tell me how deeply remorseful she was for her behaviour and actions, but in the end, it was a ruse, a way to take from me, anything of materialistic value and all she ever hunted. Once she had what she came for, she would be gone again, leaving behind a whole new path of destruction and chaotic aftermaths, whether it was in the form of breaking the law, or stealing from and defrauding me. She knew I would never turn her in. She knew that I would stand up again and blame myself. She knew that I loved her, and she used it.

But, I walked on egg shells around her. I watched every word that I said to her. I walked away from a looming argument, and I turned the other cheek when she lashed out at me. I felt safer in the presence of my tribe. There was no need to hide behind a mask around them. These were the people I learned I could trust and depend on. They were patient and kind, and made me feel as though I mattered, as though I was an exceptional and important part of their lives. Unlike my family, they didn't show up just for the good, they were there to guard me against the darkness, even though I would fail to recognize it from time to time. They never hid the truth from me, even though I sometimes didn't want to hear it. They did what my mother should have.

Finding your tribe and keeping them close is never as easy as embracing each person that walks into your life. Your tribe will be those who want to connect with you, even though you have nothing in common. What is important for your journey in The Afterwards, it to surround yourself with a tribe of powerful and supportive people who are who you needed during your abuse. It's an on-going struggle and effort not to shut them out, especially when you realize they are needed for your healing process.

You don't have to know who you are, or what your purpose in life is, you just have to be comfortable around them. Through their eyes, you will start calling back your you'ness and find yourself in a world detached from the chaos you once found yourself in.

**ALEX JONES**

# BREAKING THE CYCLE

I was so sure that I would never have the strength or emotional preparedness to bring children into my world. It was one of my greatest fears bringing innocence into a world I knew was flooded with monsters and boogeymen.

When I was unexpectedly introduced to a reality that I was about to bring a little girl into my world, I was at once flung into a darkness which left me agonizing about her safety and whether I would be able to protect her from a fate similar to mine. I instantly compared myself to my own mother and grew increasingly desperate as her birth approached.

The idea that I could break her just like my mom once broke me, weighed heavily on me. I was, after all, a broken daughter, made by a broken father, who had just escaped my broken mother. Children were never a part of my plan moving forward. I feared a repeat of the brokenness between my mother and I, but more than that, I feared that the apple might not have fallen far from the tree. Crazy thoughts entered my mind and

ALEX JONES

THE AFTERWARDS
BROKEN DAUGHTERS: MADE BY BROKEN FATHERS

overwhelmed me when I questioned whether abuse was perhaps, transferred through DNA. I questioned who I was, and who I became. I didn't trust myself, even though I could never imagine hurting another person, least of all my daughter, as severely as my mother hurt me.

In The Afterwards I said that I didn't want to hurt her or be the reason she might someday question her worth. I didn't want her to hate herself by the time she was ten years old. I didn't want her to see disgust in my eyes when she looked at me. I didn't want her to live with the knowing that she was never wanted. I didn't want her to become a lesser version of herself or hate the way she looked. I didn't want her to be a product of me.

I would fall asleep at night, terrifyingly afraid of the mistakes I was so sure I would make. Before she was born, and before I had given myself a chance with her, I was apologizing to her. Yet, from the very instant my eyes met hers, I knew without an ounce of a doubt, that there was nothing much in this world that could possibly stand in my way of my guarding her, shielding her, watching over her, or be the one to call for a war, just to keep her safe. There was nothing I wouldn't do to keep her protected, and there was nothing she could ever do where I couldn't love her. There was no one person in my world I wouldn't take on just to keep her shielded. There was nothing I wasn't prepared to do, to keep her safe from monsters and boogeymen. I was once a broken daughter, but I was not a broken mother, and I was not my mother. I once felt the same desperate need to protect my sisters, and when my daughter showed up, my need to guard and shield her from all that I had known about boogeymen and monsters, became my priority.

I was almost certain that, as she entered my world, I became a wolf myself. But, I was wrong. I didn't become a wolf when she came into my world, I was a wolf all along, and I did give up everything in an attempt to safeguard my sisters. I tried with all my might to shield them from further abuse and pain. I acted in the way my mother should have. I did for my sisters what my mother was supposed to do for us. I did for my mother, what she was supposed to do for herself. My training was complete, and although I thought I had failed miserably, I had learned the most valuable lesson I would ever learn; I was a mother.

My instincts showed up long before my daughter ever was born. As much as my life was monster and boogeyman-free at the time of her birth, it did very little to comfort me. They were still out there. They would continue to live amongst us and find a way to insert themselves into our lives. As much as I didn't want to obsess about the cruelty and evil of a world I was keenly acquainted with, I didn't want to forget or be comfortable with the idea of knowing instinctively if something like that were to happen to my daughter. I might not know. My sisters were targeted and abused, and I didn't know. I didn't see the signs I thought I would recognize anywhere. I didn't know that they were trapped in the same prison I was in, until it was almost too late. I had to remind myself that I might not know if my daughter was faced with her own monsters, until it was too late.

I needed my tribe more than ever. I needed to gather them around me so that they could teach me how to raise my little girl in a safe and functional environment. I needed guidance in creating a stable and loving home for her. I needed that from my own mother. I needed her as an example to follow and train as a mother, but, there was nothing about her I could draw from. There was nothing about her I wanted to pass on to my daughter.

It soon became clear to me that I was no longer fighting a warfare with myself. I had completed my journey to find peace with all that had happened. I had won. The world I had created for my daughter was one she was safe in. I was far better healed, than I ever was unbroken. Through my determination and bitter fight to be wonderful, she grew up in a world where I chose her over and over. There was no living or breathing human that was placed above her. She didn't know about boogeymen and monsters. She didn't know about mothers abandoning and discarding their daughters. I wanted her to trust me. I wanted her to talk to me. I wanted to be her safe place where she could run to and hide from the world when it became too much for her. I wanted to be her haven that she would find in the darkest of the night. I wanted to be her home, where she could be shielded from boogeymen and monsters should she ever encounter them. But, what it made me realize over and over again, was that I too, was once a child. Someone's little girl. I was vulnerable and fragile. I was a daughter who trusted her mother and father. I thought they loved me. My father's brutality and my mother's bitterness towards me, confused me tremendously while I was raising my daughter.

I was seeing them for who they were with a clarity I had never experienced before. I was no longer excusing my mother's behavior as that of a battered woman who had lost everything. I was no longer justifying my father's monstrous deeds due to his abuse of alcohol. For the first time, there was a kind of freedom that washed over me, that brought me the peace I was struggling to find. It wasn't me. It was them.

My shame and guilt were replaced with anger. A healthy kind of anger that helped me maintain distance from them. One where they lost their power over me. Power that was instantly transferred to me. There were moments when I felt submerged in anger for what my father had done. The rage that would flare up from time to time, left me feeling as though I should have stuck a dagger through his heart. The resentment I suddenly felt for my mother, had me questioning why she was ever allowed to bring children into her life, and into her world. I wanted to confront them and lash out at them. I wanted to let them know that the love I once felt for them, was replaced with nothing. Not hate. Not abhorrence. Not detestation. Just nothing. In its place, there where my guilt and shame lived, was now dominated by rage. I was no longer the broken daughter that burst into tears with each harsh word. I was no longer the broken daughter who hid behind my hair in an effort to become small in their world. I was no longer the broken daughter who thought I was undeserving of love and kindness. I was a mother, and an unbroken one. I was repaired, and I will never repeat.

In The Afterwards I talk about how I wanted my father to understand how much pain he was responsible for. I wanted my mother to feel what it felt like to be deemed as insignificant and branded as worthless. I wanted to know whether they could live with what they had done over so many years, and if they thought they handled The Afterwards fairly. I was stronger than the daughter they bullied, hurt and shamed. I no longer felt the punches I had absorbed from them through the years. I was never enough for them. My me'ness was never enough. My attempts to try and fix my parents, was never enough. I was the daughter who was unbroken, and it caught them entirely off-guard. I finally understood the power my mother had over me when we stepped into The Afterwards. I saw myself through her eye and evolved into the person she accused me of being. Again, I believed her when she said I was ugly, black and hard-hearted. I believed her when she said I was unable to be loved. I believed her when she said I should never have been born. I believed her when she said the abuse and The Afterwards was my fault. I believed her when she said I had brought shame into our family. I believed her when she said I was unworthy of being their daughter.

But, with each minute I was raising my daughter, I un-believed her. I began un-teaching myself all that she taught me. I finally forgave myself for any role I played in my world of monsters and boogeymen; a role I had no choice in playing.

My daughter's very existence was a guarantee that I did not "entice" my father, and I never had the power to "seduce" him. For most of my life, I kept badgering myself on the things I thought I did to bring it into our lives. I was unbroken. I was different. I would watch her sleep and know that somehow, God had sent her as an apology for my crooked world. In the blink of an eye, she rescued me. She was the me, I should have been. I became who I once needed. I became who I once yearned for, for her. I did all my mother never would, and I discarded all she did do. I ran in the opposite direction of what I knew as a child. That was my recipe for my journey as a mother, an unbroken one with unbroken motherly love.

I was a functional mother raising an unbroken daughter. Through all her choices in life, she knew me in them all. Through all the decisions she was faced with, she turned to me. Through her heartache, her sadness, her joy, her dreams and her map to her future, she knew me in them all. What I was to her, and what I did for her, she prepares to be and do for her own child. The late-night conversations we still have, the stories we still share, the encouragement I will offer her for the remainder of my life. The love I will shower her with until the end of time is evident in her approach when she welcomed her child into our world, the one I tailor-made and created for us, for my future and for hers. It is a brand-new world for me, but it is one she has always known. One I am proud of, and one, she will pass onto her children.

There are no scars, no ashes, no tears for the past, and no lingering in what was lost. It is a world that has been her haven from a chaotic world, and in turn, it has given me a chance at a normal, functional life. She will never know of a life I had once lived. Her childhood was, in her own words, perfect. When I step back and take a moment to see myself through her eyes, I see her need of me, her love and admiration for me, the respect she treats me with, but more than anything, I see her immense desire to be like me. I know that the cycle has been broken. I elected to become the mother I once needed and because of that, I was able to raise a functional, well-adjusted, wonderful human who I have no doubt, will raise another and another. I found my wonderful in her, and she found hers in me. It was the biggest secret to becoming normal and yet, it was life's simplest.

My monsters were never her cross to bear, and if I had done all else wrong in my life, the one thing I succeeded in was evolving from a broken daughter into an unbroken mother.

# THE AFTERWARDS
## BROKEN DAUGHTERS: MADE BY BROKEN FATHERS

ALEX JONES

# MOTHER KEEPS BREAKING

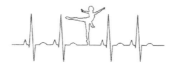

My love for my daughter has given me an overwhelming urge to keep her safe, care for her, and be present in her life. The love I have for her doesn't change the older she gets, and it doesn't release me from my responsibilities to her when she spreads her wings and flies away. I am her mother, always.

This is how it's supposed to be, right? As much as I once loved my mother, depended on her, relied on her, needed her and had faith in her, I have learned to live without her. The one thing she taught me well, was to recover from mourning her, and build a life without her in it. She taught me to live without her when I was only a little girl. She taught me to depend on myself for everything I would ever need from life. She taught me about loss. She taught me about standing alone and surviving. She taught me to live without her.

Losing her, hurt. Knowing how she felt about me, hurt. Hearing her say she can't stand to look at me, hurt. I just wanted her to see something good in me. Something she might be proud

ALEX JONES

# THE AFTERWARDS
## BROKEN DAUGHTERS: MADE BY BROKEN FATHERS

of. I wanted her to love me, so year after year, I believed her when she came back to "make amends" and fix all that was broken between us. I gave her all the second, third, fourth, and more chances in the world she said she came looking for. I wanted to believe her. I wanted to work for the love I so desperately wanted from her.

But, she wouldn't stay long, and each time she left, I felt like a failure. I felt worthless and incapable of being loved by hear. I felt incomplete and ugly. Black and hard-hearted, just like she used to say. With each slamming of the door behind her, I felt again that it was my fault, and that I again, had failed her. With each step she took in the opposite direction, she reminded me that I was not able to be loved and that not even she, my mother, could feel any connection with me.

For days after she left, I would berate myself and identify myself as her monster. As though The Afterwards was coming for me once more, I would retreat from my world each time, and punish myself incessantly. Nothing I did was right. Nothing I gave her was good enough. It didn't matter how often or how sincerely I would apologize and try to explain, it fell on deaf ears. She heard what she wanted to hear, and she did what she wanted to do. It was exhausting. It was soul crushing. It would bring me to my knees and keep me there for weeks. With each punch she would throw it me, I thought my heart would finally stop beating. I believed her again, and I believed that I was the worst of all the monsters combined. But, when I accepted that she was my only source of pain, the toxicity in my life and my home, I took the opportunity when she left for the last time, to let her go. I spent days smiling when all I wanted to do was cry. I was at war with myself once again. Then, when I replayed the years of her deceit, lies and desire to ruin me as a way to set things right with her, it was easy. It wasn't less painful, but it brought me immense peace, safety and security.

For the first time, I could see clearly, and what I did see, I hated about her. In her eyes, I owed her everything, and I deserved nothing that was good in my life. I was never supposed to crawl out of the corner she put me in. She lavished in my tears and was intimidated by my laughter. I was never supposed to recover from my monsters and boogeymen when she couldn't recover from losing my father.

I soon realized that my sisters felt the same anger and disgust for me. As much as I wanted to begin again and include my sisters, their brokenness was unrepaired. My mother wouldn't let them heal, and they believed her when she said they couldn't. They needed her. They reminded me of all that was

THE AFTERWARDS
BROKEN DAUGHTERS: MADE BY BROKEN FATHERS

wrong, and had I remained quiet and willing to do anything to keep them in my life, I would have remained broken.

I *wanted* life, and as much as I wanted a life with my mother and sisters in it, it made no difference to them. I was invisible to them. There was nothing good about me, to them.

I have life. I have my wonderful. I have found the family, joy and safety I had been searching for, all my life. What I have is beautiful, and there is no room for those hunting my destruction. As much as their words hurt me, I no longer believe them. They were wrong. Their lives no longer filter out into mine and to maintain my unbrokenness, I keep a safe distance from the brokenness they refuse to get out from.

I don't hate my mother. I pity her for living through what she did. I never once thought she would walk away from her life unscathed. It was awful for her too. My father was her monster too. I know she experienced horrific domestic abuse at his hands, and I know she suffered greatly. But, she refuses to escape the hole she has fallen into. She has no desire to climb out, discard her self-pity, and offer her daughters a way to survive. Her mind has told her that the pain her daughters have lived through, is nothing compared to her own suffering and losses. She will never believe that what we went through, could ever compare to what she suffered. My sisters pity her for it. My brother understands it. I don't.

In The Afterwards, I talk about how for most of my life, my broken mother led me to believe that I was the monster, and that I had no right to defend myself against my boogeyman. For years after, she continued degrading me emotionally because I chose to rise up and put the past behind me. The mere fact that I fought for a life I wanted to be proud of, and the result thereof that shows in my success, is almost worse than speaking out against my father. It is the most bitter pill she ever could swallow.

All I ever wanted to do, was prove that my biology does not dictate my personality, choices, successes or failures. It will never be a directive for raising my children into well-adjusted adults. It will never be the reason for my brokenness or my inability to heal. I am not the broken mother she was. I wanted those choices to be mine, not my DNA's.

I am still me. I am still the person I dreamed of becoming. I am still a good sister and daughter, only, I am no longer a sister and a daughter. I can live with that. I no longer dwell on my genetic flaws.

As mentioned in The Afterwards, my decision to remove myself entirely from my mother and the situations I found myself in around her, seemed heartless and cruel on my part for others. I have been condemned and criticized for my decision in finally letting her go, and closing my heart and home to her. I have come to terms with the fact that I had lost my mother long before The Afterwards began, and I have made peace with the reality that she is incapable of loving me.

Leading up to the complete breakup of my relationship with my mother, she noticed that I had begun changing. Almost as though in a panic, she accused me of not being the daughter I was in the years leading up to the end of our relationship. I had changed. I withdrew from her long before she ever noticed, in a desperate attempt to shield my heart from her heartless words. When I noticed her intense loathing of my daughter, I changed. I chose my journey to healing, and I chose to keep my daughter unstained. I had changed, but it wasn't a bad thing for me. For her perhaps, but not for me.

I no longer have any qualms about turning my father in. As traumatizing as The Afterwards was, it was the right thing to do. Any mother who loves her daughter, would tell her that. I had flipped that switch out of pure desperation for my sisters, my mother and myself. It was the right thing to do. It could have turned out far worse if I hadn't. I had a duty to step in for my sisters when my mother failed to. I would do it again, over and over again.

Speaking out was the hardest thing I ever had to do. Being 15 years old when I did, did not make for a softer landing. I didn't hate my parents. I thought my sister would die. I thought that eventually, my mother would be beaten to death. I spoke out not just for me, but for us all. Even for my father. I wanted him back. I wanted the monster to leave. I wanted the devil to return my father to his body. I wanted to see my father again. It will never again matter what any of them think or what they perceive the truth to be, my mother will always lead with the narrative that suits her. I will always be missing a mother. I will always need one, just not mine. Not all mothers break in The Afterwards. Not all mothers become mine. Sometimes, it still seems unfair that mine broke. Sometimes, losing them overwhelms me, but I don't dwell on it.

My mother's happy ending didn't include me, and mine didn't include anything broken.

ALEX JONES

# THE AFTERWARDS
## BROKEN DAUGHTERS: MADE BY BROKEN FATHERS

**ALEX JONES**

# A BROKEN WORLD

From as early on as I can remember, my life at home was broken and beyond repair. I can barely remember a single day that I did not have to fight against my nightmares and my monsters. My existence didn't seem fair, and my life was what my nightmares were made of.

While surviving "the thing," I thought the monster lived only in my home, and that my parents were the only monsters. The Afterwards opened my eyes to a broken world, filled with broken mothers, broken sons and daughters, and broken fathers.

All of which were confronting a demon of their own, and they were all acquainted with a boogeyman in one way or another. I was horrified to discover how broken this world was, and that I wasn't the only broken daughter turned unbroken. It was a world I fought my way through my childhood for, only to end up in a brokenness of another kind. I spent my childhood fighting against the monsters I knew, but when I began fighting

ALEX JONES

against the broken mother I didn't know, I realized that the entire world was broken.

Realizing how crooked the world was, flung me into a different kind of chaos. I couldn't hear myself anymore. My heart was disorganized, and my spirit was tainted. I couldn't understand how much cruelty there could be in a world I was fighting to belong in. It added me to the turmoil and reminded me that perhaps I did contribute to the mess. It was filled with people like me, fathers like mine, mothers similar to the one I walked away from, and families desperate to keep secrets.

Somehow, we all played a part in contributing to the pandemonium. We were all crooked. Had I been told from the very beginning that I was not responsible for our broken lives, the world I was paroled into, wouldn't have been as broken. Each time a mother rejects her child, a father hurts his son or daughter, or a child walks away from her family, the world breaks a little more. When bad behavior is influenced by enablers, right becomes wrong and wrong becomes right, the world breaks a little more.

But, it's life in a broken world where we, the broken, choose to make daily decisions to get up, dress up and show up. We un-break a little fragment each time we choose to face and conquer our obstacles. By embracing our brokenness and accepting our me'ness, work begins to un-break the fractions of us. Facing our fears, and looking our executioners in the eye, un-breaks the world a little more. Fighting evil while keeping the pieces of us intact, un-breaks what has been broken in the world. Life in a broken world is one where the powerful are idolized, and the weak are cast aside. Daughters like us are judged harshly by what our monsters did to us. We are mercilessly criticized for saving ourselves and preserving our lives.

There is something terribly broken in a world when the abused are denied healing, but support is offered to the abuser, leaving daughters with no choice but to grow up hating themselves. I hated myself and the way I looked. I hated the sound of my voice, and the way I walked or presented myself. I hated myself so much that I effortlessly placed dehumanizing labels on myself, just like my mother did. Just like the world did.

Quick did I discover that the world was not broken. My world was. Our world was. The broken daughter's was. The broken mother's was. My broken father's was. It was our world within the world that was broken. Speaking out against my father, was viewed as wrong in my broken world. Having lost my entire support system when I lost my mother and sisters, classified my world as broken. But, forgiving myself for living and

ALEX JONES

# THE AFTERWARDS
## BROKEN DAUGHTERS: MADE BY BROKEN FATHERS

surviving in a broken world, was my first step to un-breaking what was broken in my life.

The world is not broken. My world was. Instead of being struck down by "the thing" and The Afterwards, I made plans, set goals and made a conscious decision to be happy, despite it all. I couldn't change the world of the broken, but I could make mine better. And little by little, as I began accepting my new life without those I loved the most, my world started mending. The world, although still scarred and glued back together, is not as shattered as it once seemed to me.

It's a world I created away from my father's brokenness. It's a million miles away from my mother's broken life. Their world did not defeat me. The guilt I was beleaguered by, did not conquer me. The shame did not break me. "The thing" did not define me, but my broken world and those of other broken daughters very nearly did.

ALEX JONES

# ON A WING AND A PRAYER

As a child who knew nothing of monsters and boogeymen, praying was at the top of my priority list. I looked forward to my conversations with Jesus. I loved the idea that He was so close to me and listening to every word I was saying. I felt safe. Loved. Cared for. Heard.

Having conversations with Him was effortless. I knew God. My parents knew God. My father knew Him better than any of us did, and while sitting quietly in Church on a Sunday, I would listen to him speak, and hear my mother sing in the choir. I believed in angels, and I believed in God's love for us.

When "the thing" became a permanent fixture in my life, I began doubting. I still prayed. I still had my conversations with Jesus, but they were broken. It all felt so fake and far-fetched. The more I begged God to change my mother and father, the more the violence increased, and the less my mother was willing to care for us. Even though my prayers remained constant, they had no value. I promised my enduring commitment to Him. I

ALEX JONES

## THE AFTERWARDS
### BROKEN DAUGHTERS: MADE BY BROKEN FATHERS

promised obedience and silence. I promised changed behavior. I promised anything I could think of as I negotiated for our lives to be put back to the way they were.

As time went on, and as I grew a little older each year, I believed that He wasn't hearing me. He just wasn't listening to me. He had left me. Forgotten me. Perhaps, my mother was right, and I was not deserving of love. Perhaps, my heart was too dark and too hard for my prayers to reach His ears. Perhaps, I was the monster, and not my father.

I prayed. I just stopped depending on Him. My faith was lost, and hope had long since faded away. It was all that mattered to me. I thought it was important for God to step in and change my mother and father. What I saw much later was that He did step in. He did change things. He changed me.

I wasn't getting what I was asking for. I was getting what I needed to survive my broken world. I needed courage. I needed bravery. I needed to identify the fact that my mother was broken. I needed to accept that my father was gone. I needed strength. I needed to become a mother for my sisters.

I needed to listen closely and hear Him. I needed to feel His nudges. I needed to stop asking for what I wanted and see what He was giving me. I wanted an unbroken world, instead I

ALEX JONES

needed to understand that my world was not beyond repair. I wanted justice, instead I needed the strength and wisdom to forgive.

I wasn't seeing the answers to my prayers. My mother's behavior convinced me that He was absent. As her anger and disgust for me increased, I thought that God was seeing me through her eyes. I was a burden. My dreams were irrelevant. I was asking for too much. I was too small to pray for anything as big as what I was asking for. I just wanted her to love me. I wanted her to choose us over my father. I wanted her to save us. I wanted her to want to do all I was praying for.

I was so committed to seeing the answers to my prayers through my mother, that I failed to realize she was breaking my prayers. She was interfering with my relationship with God. Her hatred of me was spilling over into my conversations with Him. Once again, my desperate need to be loved and accepted by her, was stealing something of value from me.

When she taught me fear, He taught me bravery. When she taught me indifference, He taught me compassion. When she taught me betrayal, He taught me loyalty. When she taught me anger, He taught me passiveness. When she taught me selfishness, He taught me to become selfless. When she taught me hatred, He taught me affection. My mother and my monster crippled my prayers and almost, broke my spirit. Once I surrendered all she taught me, could I see all He was teaching me. Only then could I hear the answers and recognize His presence in my life from the very beginning.

There was never anything of value between my mother and I. I grew up thinking I had to earn her love. Throughout my childhood and most of my adult life, I worked tirelessly to deserve it. As the years passed, I shed many tears searching for approval from her.

What she gave me in return, was nothing more than criticism. My prayers may have been broken at some point in my life, but even then, I was given the ability to see her brokenness. I was able to hear what she never said out loud and accept the distance between us.

My prayers for my monster might have seemed unheard and undelivered for a while, but on so many nights, during so many breakdowns, it could all have ended so differently. When I thought none of us would live to see the next day, we did. When I thought the firearm against my temple would be the last thing I would ever feel, it jammed leaving my monster to give up, and walk away. When the car was headed for a brick wall at full speed

THE AFTERWARDS
BROKEN DAUGHTERS: MADE BY BROKEN FATHERS

carrying all of us, it should have struck the wall. Instead, it stopped a centimeter short.

He was there. He was listening. He knew what I needed. He *did* save me. He was never gone from me. I just didn't know what I needed.

**ALEX JONES**

# THE AFTERWARDS
## BROKEN DAUGHTERS: MADE BY BROKEN FATHERS

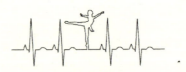

**ALEX JONES**

# ENRAGED

The problem with all the brokenness in the world is that, while overcome with rage, I never really knew who the target of my anger was. There were times when unbearable sadness evolved into an anger that entirely overwhelmed and engulfed me. Then there were times when my anger just crippled me and made way for intense sadness and emptiness.

I could never understand why my anger intensified for my mother, when it should have been directed at my father. After all, he started all this. He destroyed all that was good and sacred in our lives. He destroyed my mother. But still, my anger for her festered and progressed at an alarming rate.

I had written her a letter exposing my father but giving it to her left me feeling as though I never should have written to her. I was disappointed and extremely hurt. I was vulnerable and disillusioned by the fact that she was doing nothing to remove us from the conditions we were living in. I was crushed when I realized that it was a battle, I would be alone in fighting. It was a war I was called to, and I had no back-up. I was alone. But, my

ALEX JONES

anger and rage wasn't only directed at her. I was angry that evil found a home amongst us. Between my fear, sadness and hopelessness, I never knew what to do with the rage that would crop up more often than I was comfortable with. I was angry at the devil for wearing my father. I was bitter towards my mother for refusing to call him out. I was disgusted by the abuse. I never thought my mother wouldn't step up for us. I never once considered the fact that she wouldn't go to war with, and for us.

I was losing myself as I failed to understand why the abuse was progressing and growing increasingly violent. I watched friends and kept a close eye on their relationship with their parents. I remember riding my bicycle late one afternoon and stopped across the road from a friend's house. It wasn't dark yet, but her bedroom light was on, and her curtains were open. Her mother walked in and handed her a glass which I guessed was milk or a soda. She sat down beside her where she was doing her homework. It was ten minutes of love and affection between mother and daughter that I absolutely craved with all my being.

I couldn't help but wonder what they were talking about, and what it was that made them both laugh out loud. I envied that, and after that day, I returned almost daily just to watch the tenderness between them. It made me happy to see the devotion between them, but it kept me caught between my anger and intense sadness. I was stuck somewhere between rage, and conquered heartbreak. I desperately wanted just one of those moments with my mother. Just one.

Once in The Afterwards, I was exhausted by the grief my mother experienced losing my father and her home. She spent much time reflecting on all she had lost, and how painful it was to begin again without my father, feeling as though I gave her no choice. Her pining for my father, a man that assaulted her a hundred times before, was what turned my intense sadness into rage. Her grief was never for us, and what we went through. It was purely for what she had lost.

Bouncing around between anger and grief was as though I was standing with one foot on the side of anger, and another on the side of heartbreak. Losing my father was devastating, despite the fact that he had left the moment the monster showed up. I grieved for him from the moment the devil began wearing him. I only once voiced my desolation at missing my father, and when I was coldly reminded that it was what I had wanted, I never again dared to express my longing for him.

I was grieving my father, the man he was before "the thing." I was angry and grief-stricken by all the what-might-have-beens had the monster never stepped foot in our home, or had I never spoken out against him. For a long time in The Afterwards, I thought I acted too quickly. I was sure that with time, he might have come home. I thought that had I tolerated the abuse for just a while longer, he would come back, and restore us all to the way we were.

As far as my mother was concerned, my heartbreak was nothing more than an "act." Because I turned my father in, I had detached myself from my entire family. Listening to her condemning me, brought out turmoil in me I had never wanted to feel. But, as she condemned me to my own private hell, I began embracing and cherishing the anger I felt. I gave myself permission to feel abhorrence for her, even though she would never know.

Being angry kept me from surrendering to a broken heart. Becoming strong and allowing me to free myself from my role in my family's split, came through the anger I felt not only for my parents, but for the cruelty they inflicted upon me. Seeking my mother's approval and love, caged me and locked me away from my ability to heal. No matter what I did or ever would do, she was never going to approve of me. Knowing that I so desperately needed to hear that I did the right thing, was a tool she used to further destroy me. With that knowledge, I finally had the power to change the way I dealt with the trauma not only of the abuse, but of the rejection I felt in The Afterwards. Being angry helped me understand that it was never my fault. I no longer bowed my head in shame, instead, I looked at her and listened to her. I heard her every word and then, I reprimanded her before I walked away from her.

At first, I was afraid that my anger would eventually place me on the same level she was on. I didn't want to be so angry, that I lost myself to bitterness, and lose out on my recovery. I kept my anger at a level just enough to keep from surrendering to my heartbreak. Just enough to keep a wall between us. Just enough to survive her.

I stopped apologizing for breaking my family apart. I stopped seeking redemption for turning my father in. What my anger showed me was that I didn't need forgiveness for surviving. As time went by and realizing that I was unable to renegotiate appropriate boundaries with my parents, brought me the peace I needed. I did my best. I spent far too much time apologizing for something I was never guilty of. I cherished my anger. It would remind me of how easily I could have shifted in the opposite direction and fall into a bottomless pit of wretchedness.

As I settled into my own world free from monsters and a hateful mother, I was tempted to reach out to my sisters. But, the mere thought of hearing their voice would instantly ignite my sorrow. I had to continuously remind myself that reuniting with them would lead me to a false haven, overpowered by numbness, guilt, blame, repression and their denial of what our monster did to us.

There were times when my anger made way for desolation. Just like I had been doing for years, I wanted to surrender and apologize as much as I needed to, to bring my sisters back to me. They were a part of me, and we were sisters, once.

When The Afterwards began, I instinctively had an urge to shield and protected them. My fear for them was so overwhelming, that they felt I was smothering them. Reflecting back, I realize I was over-bearing and dictatorial. I was strict and I regularly questioned their behavior and their choices. As though they were my children, I would reprimand their bad behavior and their failure to make the rest of their lives, the very best of their lives.

Sadly, they believed all along that I owed them too, and that I had wronged both our parents. It left me engulfed by the all too familiar rage, dimmed by sadness. Because of the monster, The Afterwards has cast a long, dark shadow over our family. My mother and sisters remain captive to the past, and while I have no chains keeping me bound, I often struggle with my place in the world. Not that I don't fit in, and not that I haven't created a beautiful life for myself, but because my mother couldn't make place for me in hers.

Much of my silent rage comes from the fact that I never got the answers I so needed. My mother never could tell me what it was about me that angered her so blindly, and in turn, it fueled my anger for her. I didn't allow myself to feel the antagonism and resentment that was boiling inside of me. My pent-up anger would escape when I least expected it, and attack others who did nothing to deserve my wrath.

My world began with my mother, and for a while, my lifeline and sanctuary were with her. There is so much time in my life spent longing for emotional sustenance from her, that my years ended up slightly broken. It has always been about her, and we were a reflection of her until we weren't anymore.

For years, I felt I had no right to exist, that I was a burden to her and by her own admission, I should never have been born. And at the end of it all, her criticism and humiliation towards me was in her own words, "for my own good."

ALEX JONES

# THE AFTERWARDS
## BROKEN DAUGHTERS: MADE BY BROKEN FATHERS

So, I allow the anger to live inside of me. A healthy kind of rage just enough to shield my heart from shattering again. It keeps me alive. It keeps me optimistic in all aspects of my life. It keeps me.

**ALEX JONES**

# EVIL IS A LIAR

Right until the very end of "the thing," and at the very beginning of The Afterwards, I never thought that my mother was a willing participant of the darkness in our home. Despite the fact that she discarded my pleas for help, I still believed in her, and I believed that she would step up.

When I finally found the courage to reveal our monsters to her, I was sure that she would find a way to put an end to the abuse and remove us from my father. But, I soon discovered that evil was a liar, and all that was dark in our lives, was evil. Despite the cruelty and despite the domestic abuse she suffered at his hands, she defended him. She made excuses for his behavior, and then, she criticized me for finding my voice.

The fact that she mothered four children was a promise I assumed she made to nurture and care for us. A promise I desperately relied on, and not for one moment, did I doubt or question her priorities. I never thought that it was wrong to presume we would be safe once she knew the truth. But, like

ALEX JONES

most things in our lives at the time, she left us with something else that was broken, broken promises and lies. She turned the tables on me, and accused me of being imbalanced, selfish, spiteful, spoilt with a tendency to overreact. Even though I always felt that the darkness was not limited only to my father, but my mother too, I constantly berated myself for judging her so harshly, when she was a victim of domestic abuse.

As the years into The Afterwards passed, I identified new and unexpected lies and realized, she was out for revenge. She wanted "justice" from me for speaking out and turning my father in. She wanted payback for all that she had lost, and she was determined to collect. By then, the idea of having a mother was gone. In her place was something evil, desperate to own my accomplishments while constantly berating and insulting my efforts.

When she thought I had something of value to offer her, she would lie her way back into my life by assuring me that she was changed, and she loved me. She would go on to subtly remind me of all that she had lost, and that her world was far too cruel and unkind for her to function in. She saw no other way than to end her own life. In her mind, there was no reason to carry on living when the life she had and loved, was stolen from her. I had stolen it all from us all. She again reminded me that she had "sacrificed" everything for me, and as a result, I felt indebted to her which ended up commanding my obedience and loyalty to her. She left me with a false sense of security while professing her love for me, before withdrawing her kindness and affection from me the moment I refused to surrender to her desires. I was caught up in her lies and confused by her love. It felt as though I had to constantly prove my love and worth to her.

Through her patience and lies, I never once considered the fact that revenge was her ultimate goal and greatest victory. Each time she came back, the cycle would begin almost exactly as it did the last time. I still, never saw it until it was too late. When she finally left like a thief in the night each time, she left my finances and heart in a mess for months after.

The Boogeyman was no better. My father understood the guilt I felt for turning him in. He knew that at one point, I would have done almost anything to get a do-over and change that one moment in my life when "I destroyed our home." It took me many years to make peace with turning him in, but until then, his darkness had never diminished. Like my mother, he was out for revenge. When we finally managed to resolve to work on our relationship by promising that he was no longer the monster I knew, he presented me with a statement to sign. One in which I "admit to lying about the abuse." I was devastated. I thought he

# THE AFTERWARDS
## BROKEN DAUGHTERS: MADE BY BROKEN FATHERS

was taking responsibility for what he had done. He led me to believe that he was sorry, and that he wanted a second chance to be the father I deserved. He made me understand that the monster living inside of him, was gone. I believed him. I wanted so badly to believe him, because I still loved him. All I ever wanted was for my father to come back, and when I thought he did, he lied. I was crushed by the fact that he wanted me to lie and take back the years of cruelty. It was never clearer to me than at that very moment, that the devil still wore my father. He was a liar. Evil is a liar. His carefully laid out plans were in full effect, and when I gathered what was left of my heart, I quietly walked away.

Still, I wasn't ready to let go of my mother or sisters. A few months after her leaving, she would be back. Each time she walked into my home and my life, she would immediately take control and manipulate me with new promises, all of which were broken. Each time she came back, she would set a brand-new trap for me to fall into.

Still, she found a way to question my standards which turned out to be lower than hers. Whatever I took on, she would demean and find fault with anything I did. More than anything, she was horrified by my parenting skills, and would constantly harass me about having no mothering instincts whatsoever. It would often slip out that there "was something wrong with me."

ALEX JONES

# THE AFTERWARDS
## BROKEN DAUGHTERS: MADE BY BROKEN FATHERS

Again, self-doubt overwhelmed me. More often than not, I remained silent because the moment I voiced my disapproval, she would become enraged and accuse me of disrespecting her and questioning her motives. Even when her mistakes came to the surface, she refused to take responsibility for her actions. It was never her fault, but rather, the result of something I had done. What the outside world saw was intelligence, someone who was highly educated and extremely well spoken. The world praised a wonderful mother, and pitied her, her problem child. Me.

The child that no-one could love. The ugly, black and hard-hearted daughter who set out to destroy her family. They were quick to point out that I should have been grateful that she so much as stomached me. When enough time had passed, I began realizing that she was not my mother anymore. I doubted if she ever was. There were more monsters in my world than I cared to admit to. Her abuse of me was never physical, but the emotional suffering she put me through, inflicting endless damage to me and my home, was at times, almost worse than the physical, sexual abuse.

Her lies were nothing more than a foot in my door. Her emotional and verbal cruelty against me, was crippling. Her sense of entitlement was shocking, and her lack of empathy was unbelievable. She was ruthless and without conscience. When I began adjusting to The Afterwards by diligently creating a life I could be proud of, her shaming of me intensified. Her lies were so great, I could no longer identify when she was lying, or when she was telling the truth.

In The Afterwards, I said that I thought the most astounding of all were her comparisons of my sisters and I. My appearance made me ugly, my disobedience made my repulsive and my accomplishments were unremarkable, leaving my self-worth to continue to plummet. My sisters were extensions of her, I wasn't. My sisters were controlled, I couldn't be. They were untainted, where I was rotten to the core. As far back as I can remember, she would reward good behavior by lavishing beautiful and expensive clothes and gifts on my sisters, and I, on the other hand, got only what I needed.

By detaching myself and my life from her and her lies, I was able to break the cycle, and remove myself from the clutches of evil. As easy as it should have been, it wasn't. I grieved losing her and my sisters. It was never what I planned to do or ever wanted. In the years after The Afterwards began, I was never able to create boundaries between my mother and my life. I tolerated my own discomfort in an effort to mend my relationship with her. I did a lot of feigning, especially pretending to be someone I wasn't. I had to fake my emotions and bite my tongue whenever she was close by. More than anything, I had to learn to see myself through the eyes of those who stuck around for me. Often, it would stun me when someone handed me a compliment. I did not quite believe my partner when he would remark that I was beautiful, or that I dressed beautifully, or that I was a good person. Evil is a liar.

ALEX JONES

# THE AFTERWARDS
## BROKEN DAUGHTERS: MADE BY BROKEN FATHERS

**ALEX JONES**

# MY ME'NESS, YOUR YOU'NESS

Because I could never quite pinpoint when it was that there was a breakdown of the relationship between my mother and I, I kept wanting to be someone else in a desperate attempt to gain her approval, desperately hoping that the world would be more accepting of me. I would watch my mother's reaction to a friend's daughter, or an acquaintance from Church's daughter, and when my mother was taken by her, I would study the daughter closely. I would watch her every move, hear her every word, and scrutinize her behavior.

I would learn all there was about her so that I could transform into her. Be like her. Talk like her. Walk like her. Dress like her. Act like her and behave like her. I would discard all that I liked and make her hobbies my own. I left my swimming team to take up athletics, even though I was awful at it. I left ballet to take up horse-riding, which didn't turn out too badly. I listened to the music she liked, and I watched movies she enjoyed. I became someone else, over and over again. I no longer knew

ALEX JONES

whether I preferred dresses or jeans. Did I like sandals or running shoes? I couldn't even tell you what food I enjoyed, or what color I liked. I lost me. By desperately trying to transform into someone else, I lost my me'ness. Each time I had successfully transitioned into someone else, it made no difference to my mother, and as a result, I would pick out someone else. It was exhausting. It was soul-crushing and stole my me'ness from me.

I would find myself staring at my mother when she wasn't looking. I admired her beauty. I looked nothing like her. She was dark, I was fair. She was short, I was tall. She was beautiful, I was ugly. When she wasn't home, I would sneak into her closet, and admire her beautiful dresses and collection of shoes. Her perfume was what I would always recognize about her, and I daydreamed of becoming her someday.

She was all I wasn't or could ever be. I idolized her and hung on her every word. I wanted to be just like her, instead, I turned out to be nothing like her. I turned into the complete opposite version of her. I don't own a dress or a skirt. I am happiest when I am barefoot, but if I do need to put shoes on, they are running shoes. I can't stand the smell of perfume and have never owned a bottle. I like the me I was as a child, and I like the me I have become. That me'ness is mine. As wholeheartedly as I accepted my mother for who she was, despite all her

ALEX JONES

mistakes, she could never extend me the same courtesy. She stole my me'ness from me as a child, and as hard as I tried to be the daughter I thought would be enough, the more significantly our relationship deteriorated. There was never really one big thing that caused division between us, it was a million little things. It was a million little things that showed me how broken we were. Each time I tried to mend our relationship, I lost a little more of myself, but I thought it might change the horrors of my childhood. I thought I'd be able to understand her role in it all, and her disassociation from me. Only once I started calling the real me back, did I realize that it was always good enough. It was what kept me alive. My me'ness is what saved me. My determination to be better and wonderful, was me, not someone else I evolved into. My ability to conquer the monsters, came from the real me. Overcoming a shattered heart, and functioning normally in a crooked world, was all me. Me. My me'ness.

I once again paid attention to my emotions, my thoughts and my approach to my world. I was intensely aware of the peace that had come into my mind, and into my life. I had taken me back. I had embraced who I was, what happened to me, and how I survived it all. I let go of all that wanted to change and destroy me. I was stronger, and braver as me, than I ever was as someone I tried to become. While trying so desperately to become

ALEX JONES

someone else, I was afraid to do much of anything out of fear of failing. I would work behind closed doors, and practice where no-one could see me until I felt I had mastered whatever it was that I was attempting. I had lost who I was, and I was struggling with who I thought I wanted to be, and as a result, I was my own harshest critic, and worst enemy.          The time I spent trying to be someone else, someone the world could love and approve of, left me with some of my worst memories. But, my life without my mother gave me an opportunity to find myself again, and discover my me'ness instead of creating a me she could be proud of.          Time has given me peace and acceptance. I have peace with all of me, even the parts that were once broken, but glued together so well, you could hardly see it. I am not perfect. I am not better or superior to them, but I am me. Some parts of my me'ness may not be to everyone's taste, and other parts might need a lot more work, but it is me and who I am. It is what keeps my surviving. It is what has nudged me and led me through some of my darkest days and nights. It is me, unbroken.

**ALEX JONES**

# THE HOURS THAT TICK BY

So much time was spent on self-doubt, shame, guilt, self-hatred and trying to find just one thing that was good about me. The hours that ticked by left me unable to truly find the answers I thought I needed and kept me frustrated and unable to truly move forward.

But, because of the mercy time brought me, I have learned to let go of the anger, resentment and pity I was drowning in. Anger for myself, unable to be who I thought I should be. Resentment for those expecting too much from me, and self-pity because I thought I was just not strong enough. The hours that ticked by, brought me closer to a time in my life when that which once crushed me, no longer had the power to hurt me.

Through the passage of time, I no longer linger in the notion that fences need mending. Some things are broken, and sometimes, they are meant to stay broken. Because of the hours that tick by, we don't qualify for do-overs. We can't go back and

ALEX JONES

do things differently. We can't change bad behavior in others, and we can't always put relationships back to the way they were before. So much time is spent on coping with abuse, and the after-effects thereof. We linger, desperate to pick up the pieces that have been shattered. We waste these hours in apologizing for things we were never guilty of. And then, we spend more time doubting ourselves, shaming ourselves, blaming ourselves and hating ourselves.

But, the hours that tick by brings something else with it. Healing. It brings comfort and allows us to let go of all that seeks to destroy us. It brings wisdom, and it gives us new eyes to see what we couldn't see sooner. We hear differently. We see clearly. We feel otherwise, and we find trust in ourselves and others again. We are different as the hours tick by.

During "the thing," time felt like it had stood still. The days were extremely long, and the nights would sometimes never end. I had my eye on growing up, and leaving, but time was unkind. The hours just never seemed to tick by. When I walked into The Afterwards, not only was time slow, but it was incredibly cruel. As much as I wanted to go back to the day I turned my father in, I couldn't. I couldn't change the outcome of our lives, because the hours had in fact, ticked by. As much as I hated time, I realized that it was never about waiting for someone to save us.

ALEX JONES

# THE AFTERWARDS
## BROKEN DAUGHTERS: MADE BY BROKEN FATHERS

Time had given me an opportunity to grow stronger, until I found the courage to draw the line, and reveal our monsters. Even though much of my hours were stolen because too much of it was spent in fear, it was all part of the plan to raise me and give me the courage to find my voice.

What once seemed as lost time to me, were hours I functioned in, and grew up in. I didn't lose time, even though my childhood was lost. I lived. I was alive. I breathed. I survived the hours that ticked by. It was broken, but it trained me, and taught me to do what I never thought I could. It led me to a moment that saved us even if I couldn't see it at the time.

As kind as time was in the later years, I couldn't ignore the cruelty that led up to it. So much of the hours that ticked by was spent in shock once we slipped into The Afterwards. It was a time where everything around us came crashing down on us, while the world carried on turning, and time carried on ticking by so slowly, as though The Afterwards was just a stranger in their world.

Each hour that plummeted me into a battle with my own demons, was an hour that left me feeling increasingly hopeless and distraught. There were hours that would swallow me whole, leaving me feeling as though I was drowning in my own grief and

ALEX JONES

# THE AFTERWARDS
## BROKEN DAUGHTERS: MADE BY BROKEN FATHERS

devastation. These were the hours that I could think of nothing else but how broken our lives were. I didn't just feel alone, I was alone with nowhere to run to and no-one to confide in. Time was suffocating me when each day was nothing more than a repeat of the day before. Nothing was different. Nothing was changing. The anger was the same. The heartache was the same. The blame was the same. Each hour of each day was the same. Time was not passing, and I was not able to move on. It felt as though I was stuck in the hands of time that weren't moving.

I watched the hours tick by for the rest of the world. While mine wasn't, the sun still continued to rise and set on schedule. The birds woke up in the mornings, and their songs were perfectly sung each day. People were coming and going. Children were rushing to school, and cars were driving through the streets and the highways. It was normal. Their hours were ticking by, while I was frozen in the hours of a clock that was broken.

It might have been slightly off-center, perhaps a few hours off, but with each foot I placed in front of the other, life continued to move forward, and my hours continued to tick by. With each moment of acceptance, and with each recalling of my me'ness, the hours began ticking by normally. The heartache remained, the silent tears continued to fall, but it was perfectly

ALEX JONES

in tune with the hours that ticked by. The cruel years were suddenly gone, and the clock that was broken would never be a clock that was never broken, but it has taken me to a time where normal is now on my time. Being so focused on blaming time and demanding a do-over, I was trapped in the past, unable to let go, and unable to allow time to bring what I needed the most, healing. I thought that going back and changing the outcome would heal me. I thought that revisiting my childhood, and ridding our home of the boogeyman, was what I needed to move in perfect synchronicity with time. I thought I had to go back and do things differently. I wanted to erase the time spent fearing my boogeyman.

I wanted to destroy him and expunge the years I suffered under him. But, time doesn't go back. The hours never tick in reverse. I could never go back, but I could move forward. I could embrace the time that was and look forward to the hours that would tick by from that moment on.

For each hour I spend navigating The Afterwards, I remind myself that the time spent surviving my father, and then my mother, was time well spent. It may have been broken, but it is precious time that is denied to many like me. Others had no time at all. Their monsters stole any chance of any more hours to tick by. Their time was lost to them. Forever. Even though my

# THE AFTERWARDS
## BROKEN DAUGHTERS: MADE BY BROKEN FATHERS

time was slow and slightly broken, it was a time in which I was able to learn to live again. It changed me, and it raised me. It helped me find my me'ness again, and it gave me a voice, even though it sometimes still shudders and shakes.

My clock was once broken, but now that it is repaired, I cherish the moments ahead of me, and even those behind me. I have dreamed of building a life where time is the most valuable of all. The hours that ticked by allowed me to listen to and identify that which serves me.

What I do know is that we, people like you and me, were called to a war, many others weren't. That makes the time spent fighting off our monsters and boogeymen pretty significant.

**ALEX JONES**

# THE WAR WE WERE CALLED TO

In the beginning of "the thing," I was too afraid to fight off my boogeyman, my father. I didn't fully understand what was happening or that it would happen well into my teens. I loved my father. He was my larger-than-life superman, and the first I had ever loved. I didn't want to fight him, and I didn't want to disappoint him. I was a good girl. I was his little girl, so I surrendered and obeyed when he commanded my nights.

It was terrifying, and I was exhausted by the warfare taking place inside of me. I felt defeated and alone. My prayers weren't changing anything, and as a result, I felt forgotten. My father was becoming increasingly violent and volatile by the day, and the monsters he would bring to me from time to time, appeared more frequently at night.

I began negotiating with God, making deals and promises to Him, if He were to rescue us. I was desperate to negotiate my freedom, but I felt as though I was under His radar. The harder I prayed, the darker my nights were and eventually, I stopped

ALEX JONES

praying, hoping or having faith that time would pass where I would finally grow up and be free. I wanted a way out of my world. I wanted to fall asleep, and never wake up again. There was nothing but emptiness inside of me, and I became numb. Desensitized. I was okay with that. It helped me cope with the physical and emotional torment going on inside of me. I didn't even want to fight it anymore. Each night my boogeyman and monsters would close my bedroom door behind them, I would lay into the early hours of the morning trying to plan a way out.

In The Afterwards, there were times that the emotional torment was a thousand times worse than the physical abuse of "the thing." The monster had changed faces and names, and my mother was my new nightmare. It was when I wanted a way out more than I wanted a way out of "the thing."

Somehow, I clung to life, and with each day that I put off removing myself from my world, I became progressively determined to survive. I knew I couldn't wait for the impossible to happen. I couldn't count on my mother to come in like a knight in shining armour, gather us in her arms, and take us away to a new world; one where we would have no contact with, or memory of our monsters. I realized that I could never change what had happened, or the darkness that was still surrounding us. I couldn't linger in a world I was barely surviving in, hoping and praying for a way out. I couldn't wait for someone to rescue me, and even though I thought I couldn't change the way I dealt with any of it, I did. My warfare was not over yet, and to pick up my fight, I stopped dreaming of all the could-have-beens, the what-ifs, the memory we, as a family could have made. It was wat it was, and it will always be what it was. I was grieving my family. I was grieving the life we should have had. I was mourning the parents they should have been.

Keeping myself a step back and locked in the past, brought me to a new kind of darkness only I was responsible for. I was to blame for being unable to look my life squarely in the eye and find the courage to move on. It was not up to God, or my parents, or the boogeymen and monsters, it was up to me with a lot of help from God. He hadn't forgotten me. He was sending messages I was too absorbed in my own pain, to listen to. I was becoming my own worst enemy by not getting up and walk into the unknown ahead of me.

For the first decade into The Afterwards, I did all I could do to make myself invisible. I didn't want anybody to see me. Even though I had a floodgate of emotions inside of me, and adequate words to silence my mother, I didn't. Instead, I defended her attacks against me. I didn't want to be a burden to her any longer. Her heartache and tears were already a cross I

## THE AFTERWARDS
### BROKEN DAUGHTERS: MADE BY BROKEN FATHERS

was bearing. Each time she would hurl hurtful accusations at me, banishing me to a hell I knew I was already living, I thought I deserved it. I was exhausted by not fighting for me. I was tired of making it my number one priority to change who I was in order to seek the world's approval. I was waiting for permission from the world to survive. To live. To choose life. After the first time I defended myself, it was easier the next time. And the time after that. She became angrier and increasingly uncomfortable in my presence, the stronger I appeared before her. It was clear that my me'ness was taking up a space in her life, she wanted gone. My self-care and healing were a priority to me, but one she was never ready for.

While caught up in my own darkness and sorrow, and while unwilling to defend myself, my mother had immense power over me. I was fading into the background the louder, more resentful and hurtful she became. It made her happy and allowed her to shine while I surrendered to her every demand.

I felt like I was wearing the devil, but as the hours ticked by, I realized that I didn't need a broken mother. I needed a mother, just not mine. She didn't need me either. I was everything she hated, and all she couldn't stand to look at. I was the anger in her words, the pain in her tears, the hurt in her heart, and the claws in her soul. What was supposed to mould and grow

ALEX JONES

me, broke me. All that she was, turned out to be all that I never wanted to be. For a long time, I thought I was walking away from her, my mother, but, I was walking away from so much more. I was walking away from resentment, hatred and confrontations that hurt and angered me. I walked away from a woman who chose to devalue and demoralize me.

The only warfare I had to engage in, was one in which I had to walk away from a mother who undermined my peace. It was time to remove myself from her judgements and the fear that would hold me captive for eternity if I didn't. My world with my monsters in it, was exhausting. An Afterwards that included a new monster, was demoralizing to a point that I could no longer see a life that was worth living, or a world that was worth living in. Their presence brought about an unhealthy kind of anger, a crushing kind of sadness and immense shame for who I was, what I had done, and what had happened to me. I was trapped in a cycle where I was responsible for fixing all the players of a cruel and wicked game, and then, absorb the punches thrown at me.

Not only was I controlled by my father during "the thing," but I was controlled by my mother, sisters, and extended family in The Afterwards. My version of the truth was never the version they wanted to hear. Each had their own sequence of events, and it was so far removed from mine that there were times I thought

## THE AFTERWARDS
### BROKEN DAUGHTERS: MADE BY BROKEN FATHERS

I was wrong. I thought I had imagined it all. I thought I was losing my mind. I thought there was something psychologically wrong with me. But, when I remember my fear, when I still find myself watching my bedroom door handle at night, and when I think back to the circles drawn in the palm of my hand, I know into the very core of me that my truth is the truth. It was always my truth and it will always be the truth. Even if it differs from my mother and sisters, and even if my father denies the years of monsters and boogeymen, I lived it, and I lived every moment of it.

We were all casualties of a war. We were all engaged in some kind of warfare, and we were all feeling the terrors of it. But, what I wasn't prepared for was that mine would include a lifetime of being reminded that I should never have been born.

My most insignificant flaws were perceived as my greatest imperfections, and it would be thrown at me by dragging up our past continuously. I would constantly be reminded of the greatness my mother once was, and that I had single-handedly managed to steal it from her. My strength was drawn from the warfare inside of me, and it was a kind of strength I never knew I had. It was what ultimately showed me the truth, and introduced me to a mother's conditional love, one I still can't quite understand. She has shown me that she would go to the end of the earth to protect her shortcomings, and she would willingly

# THE AFTERWARDS
## BROKEN DAUGHTERS: MADE BY BROKEN FATHERS

manipulate all into attacking my credibility. That was the fight in me that once broke, until I realized that she wouldn't always have the power to hurt me as much. My life would mean something someday, if only to me, and it could be good again. The impenetrable wall I found between my mother and I, was a blessing I have been thankful for every day since. It's better she stays behind it.

**ALEX JONES**

# THE AFTERWARDS
## BROKEN DAUGHTERS: MADE BY BROKEN FATHERS

**ALEX JONES**

# GUARD UP

Saving myself and my sisters was a kind of responsibility I gave myself to save us from our monsters, and it was something I never asked for, and never wanted. I placed myself in a position to fight against those who I believed would help us and love us. I saw a broken mother I had never really taken notice of, but one I never thought could break. As rocky as our relationship was during "the thing," I wholeheartedly believed she would save us, defend us and protect us.

When I discovered the lie I had been living with for so many years, it shook me to the core. I wandered around aimlessly for days on end feeling as though I might have misunderstood, or perhaps, she would snap out of it the moment the shock wore off. I didn't want to believe that she wouldn't help us. I couldn't. I just couldn't. After a while, I questioned everything I thought I knew about my mother, and our family as a whole. In an instant, my guard was up. I lost faith in her, and I didn't trust her with anything anymore. It wasn't a gradual process, instead, from the

ALEX JONES

# THE AFTERWARDS
## BROKEN DAUGHTERS: MADE BY BROKEN FATHERS

moment I handed her a letter, and her unexpected response to it, my guard was up. She was mad at me. Not my father. Not the monsters of the night. Not what they were doing, or that they were responsible for my sister's seizures. She was mad at me.

I stepped into The Afterwards with evidence from "the thing" that I could never let my guard down around her. A guard had been in place for years against my father, and I knew he was never going to show up and banish our boogeymen or monsters. I reluctantly found peace in the devil wearing my father, and I had grieved his leaving. My guard was up. I knew it wasn't him, and I knew he was probably never coming back.

I didn't see that with my mother. I didn't consider a world where she would defend my father, and his actions. I didn't see it coming. I didn't think there was ever a reason anyone could come up with, to justify the nightly visits. Yet, she did. I looked at her differently and have never quite been able to identify her as my mother after that. But, it wasn't only her.

It was the world we were living in and the people who were a part of our world. The reactions were the same from everyone around me. Some didn't say anything at all, and avoided stories about monsters and boogeymen at all cost. Others whispered quietly when they peered in my direction. The look on their faces told a million stories of disgust and revolt for me. But others would ask questions, so many questions over and over again. The same questions. New questions. Old questions. These were questions designed to catch me in a lie. If one word was out of place, it was victory, even though the story was always the same. It scared me, and finally helped me build a wall around me.

I was tremendously guarded against others. Even though the future helped me remove brick by brick of this wall, it still remained shaky and suspicion has always been a trait I have had trouble shaking. I quickly understood that when I was being treated as someone insignificant, I was inconsequential to them. When I wasn't important enough to care about, I believed them. After all, if my mother couldn't care, how could anyone else, right?

The years that followed was somehow an extension to the lesson I had learned many years before. The faith and conviction I had in not only my mother, but those closest to me was the foundation to which I clung. I thought it would be unshaken, and unbroken. I thought that I could survive anything, even my monsters. When it all began crumbling around me, all hope I had for a safer life, was gone. I didn't want to turn my father in. I didn't want him to leave. I just wanted him back. I wanted "the thing" to be over. I never wanted to speak of it again. Instead, speaking out and turning him in was all I felt I could do, and it broke my mother's heart. It bróke the hearts of our family and the people in our world. We never spoke of "the thing," or what we had to endure night after night. We never discussed what led me to turn him in, and I never had the opportunity to explain why I had made such a drastic decision.

What was discussed as the hours ticked by was what my mother and family had suffered. It was about her broken life, and that of my sisters. Not once has she ever validated the fact that we had a right to a safer, healthier and functional life. Believing that my mother would be my greatest supporter during my darkest hours, was my biggest mistake. Simply because I loved her above all, didn't mean she loved me back. Because I thought she would fight for us and our freedom from the nightmares at home, didn't mean she would. Trusting her not to abandon me was ignorance on my part. Her remarks were crushing. Her accusations were shattering. Her bitterness was all-consuming.

For a while, she had the power to shape me by first abandoning me, and then her controlling me. When my guard came up, I realized that it was just one more way to "get back at me" for ruining her life. I had long since learned to read between the lines since nothing she really said could be trusted. I believed that she would follow the rules and use the authority she had over my life in a way any normal mother would. I didn't understand much about what was right or what was wrong. I couldn't possibly know what choices to make, or what was normal and what was not, but I trusted my mother to know and to choose right over wrong. Following her lead, was impossible. She was missing.

The decisions I made; were choices I didn't want to make. I didn't want to be responsible for decisions that might have been wrong. I didn't want the world to know about our world that was home to boogeymen and monsters. I just wanted her to fix it. I wanted her to stop it. I wanted her to free us from the clutches of evil. I never expected my mother to understand, forgive me or love me simply because she felt she was compelled to. I needed her to understand what we had been through and why I had spoken out against my father. I wanted her to forgive me for the distrust I had in her, and I wanted her to do it all because she loved me as I had loved her. The rules I was taught as a child, were rules I thought she'd follow, not because she had to, but because it appeared to be what was best for her children. I wanted her love and acceptance, because then I might have been able to forgive, and love myself a whole lot sooner. She was given the power to change the way we saw ourselves. The power to

## THE AFTERWARDS
### BROKEN DAUGHTERS: MADE BY BROKEN FATHERS

protect us and take responsibility for us. She chose differently, and not once has she expressed regret or remorse. Not once has she surrendered to the idea that perhaps, the life we were flung into by "the thing," was as harsh and cruel as we claimed it to be. Not once has she considered her actions in The Afterwards, and how it was the root of ongoing inner turmoil and struggles that were cruel and unkind.

I thought that when the shock wore off, she would validate my fear, broken heart and actions I took out of desperation. I thought she would identify and concede to the darkness in our home and agree that we were presented with evil. All I ever wanted from her was to tell me that I didn't lure out the monsters, and that it was never my fault. With my guard up, I learned to let go of my desperate need to understand her. I was not a priority to her, and I was able to let go of the fear of losing her. I could trust myself, and walking away from her, our world and the darkness, was always the right thing to do.

ALEX JONES

# NO SURRENDER

Writing that letter to my mother where she would learn of our detailed, nightly encounters with the devil that wore my father, was one of the hardest things I have ever had to do. I couldn't find the words, and when I did, it seemed too harsh to present to her. I re-wrote that letter in a dozen different ways, before I realized that no matter how I would ever word it, it would never be less cruel. It would always be something no-one would ever want to read.

For days, I walked around with the letter tucked away in my pocket or kept under my pillow as I desperately tried to find the courage to give it to her. Unable to go through with slipping the note in her hand, I would crumple it, determined to throw it away, but unable to.

I wrote her about the boogeymen and monsters. I tried to reassure her that it wasn't our father, but rather the devil wearing him. I asked her not to be sad, but that he had left us a long time ago, and that he might still be in there somewhere. I

ALEX JONES

THE AFTERWARDS
BROKEN DAUGHTERS: MADE BY BROKEN FATHERS

was sure that once the monsters were revealed, he would come back to us.

I hurriedly wrote about the door handle that turned at night, but that I tried to hide. It didn't matter where I hid, he still found me. Sometimes, other monsters were with him, and once, I counted four. I begged her not to be sad because I was okay, but that my sister Lily, wasn't. I tried to explain that I was sure the boogeyman was what was making her sick, and the reason for her seizures. I asked her if she had noticed that Lisa was hiding and crying somewhere inside of her.

I said that we could hear him beat her, and we'd listen to her crying at night. Couldn't she please stop him? I was so afraid that he might kill her, and then, us. I mentioned the firearm he kept hidden in his closet, and how often he brought it into my bedroom to remind me to keep our secret. I told her I had learned how to use it. I told her that I didn't want my sisters to die.

I begged her not to leave us behind when she went to the grocery store, or Church because that was when he did things too. I told her that sometimes, I could feel my heart beating so loudly that I hoped she could hear. I told her that I wanted my father back, and that I wanted my sisters to live. I told her that as much as I wanted to run away from it all, I couldn't move. I was

ALEX JONES

frozen. I couldn't fight. I was paralyzed. It was as though I was being slammed into invisible barriers all around me and that the piercing moaning of the boogeyman made it hard to breathe. I told her that the devil was living amongst us. I told her that I hated him and living one more moment with him would only guarantee more hatred, betrayal, hostility and pain. I told her that I knew she didn't know, and that I knew she didn't hear our screams. They were silent, bouncing around inside of us. I asked her to help us stop it, because I couldn't stand one more night in the darkness. And then, I wrote about how truly sorry I was, and how I wished we could go back to before.

Writing that letter, and then giving it to my mother turned into the single biggest regret of my life. It turned out to be the day I realized with shock that she knew and perhaps, she just didn't want to admit it. Instead, she showed my father the letter. He read each word I wrote about the devil, boogeymen and monsters. He read about my vulnerability and fear. She betrayed me. She betrayed my sisters. She betrayed herself.

Giving him the letter, made way for more violence, aggression and distrust. She knew him well enough to know that showing him my letter would make way for anger and open the door to punishment. I confided in her and in return, she left me feeling confused, ashamed and guilty. She was not my mother;

she was someone bad for me. He was not my father; he was the boogeyman. Still, instead of surrendering to the betrayal, I reached a point of not surrendering at all. It was a life I was a part of in that moment, but it was never who I would become. It was a life in which I felt lost and alone. I lost sight of the fight when I thought I couldn't battle the devil without my mother. I needed her bravery and strength. I needed her guidance. I thought I needed her for life to be whole again.

Still, after coming to terms with her betrayal, I knew I couldn't surrender. I fought against the life I was born into. I struggled from that moment on to become better, and I made a conscious decision to do the right thing, all the time. My only goal was to have others recognize that my broken life as a child, did not dictate my life as an adult. No surrender. Ever.

My father was a master manipulator, a drunk and an abuser. He was a monster who had invaded all that was once good about him. My mother was and will remain vain and self-loving. My sisters have since refused to acknowledge and recognize the darkness that was once around us, and after all the years, they continue to defend my mother's behaviour. They have surrendered to their past. By not surrendering to any sort of victimhood, I have remained composed while my sisters developed resentment and antagonism towards society. They

ALEX JONES

have embarked upon an unhealthy path of anger towards the world and everyone in it, everyone but our parents. They were left blinded by the darkness that had surrounded us, and they refused to consider a reality in which our lives were broken by our father, and then again, by our mother. No surrender was as simple as rejecting feelings of self-pity and indignity that my mother had tried to instil in me. As much as a understood that I alone was responsible for my actions and who I would become someday, I had to remind myself that it was my responsibility to fit into a world that didn't know of boogeymen and monsters.

The world owed me nothing more than what I was willing to work for. The world was not at fault for the devil that wore my father. I was given a choice to recover, repair and never repeat. I took it.

ALEX JONES

# THE AFTERWARDS
## BROKEN DAUGHTERS: MADE BY BROKEN FATHERS

**ALEX JONES**

# FORGIVING YOU, FIRST

During The Afterwards, I found myself walking between a very fine line of abhorrence for myself, and revolt for others. When I was able to forgive myself, I was unable to forgive others. It would bring about a kind of turmoil inside of me that led me to unforgiving myself just so that I could forgive my parents, and those who were fixtures in my world.

It wasn't that I wasn't willing to forgive myself and others, it just didn't allow me to. When I thought I was wrong, or blamed myself for not only "the thing," but for The Afterwards, I forgave others for what I had done. But there were times when I knew that my survival depended on turning my father in, and then, I forgave myself. I was constantly forgiving and unforgiving myself, and my world.

When I realized that the anger I felt for my mother was justified, I was able to forgive me first. It was easy when I understood that she never needed any kind of exoneration from me, or from my sisters, and that she had no remorse for her

ALEX JONES

unwillingness to help us. I could live with unforgiving her and forgiving me first. Before, I was caught up with the idea that she couldn't help us because of the shock, and the fear she felt for my father. I thought she wasn't strong enough, and didn't quite know how to move forward, and rescue us.

Still, as mentioned before, I continue to linger with a fair amount of anger, I struggle to let go of. For that, I have forgiven myself, but because of that, I am torn between forgiving and unforgiving the enablers of my past encounters with boogeymen and monsters.

Enablers who don't take responsibility for "the thing" or The Afterwards. For some inexplicable reason, I am no longer angered or bare much, if any resentment towards my father. Forgiving him was easy, after all, my mind still won't let me believe it was him. Forgiving him was only possible once I decided I didn't have to love him. I didn't have to see him again. I would never have to hear his voice again.

My mother on the other hand, is no longer as valuable in my life as I thought she once was. She can contribute nothing of essence to me or to my world. Accepting the anger I have for her, is harder than I ever thought it would be, but it has helped me live in my own skin, even though I no longer place pressure on myself to forgive her. "The thing" happened to her, not us as a whole. Forgiving those who never needed forgiveness, deserves none.

I can live with my anger and occasional bouts of unforgiveness, so can she. I have learned to accept that she truly believes what she chooses to believe. Her heart and mind believes her truth while I am at ease with mine. I could never love her again as I once did and should. I was left to stand alone. I was left to navigate the world alone while trying to create a world I could function in and be proud of.

Just like each one of them had to, I had to navigate my way through a broken life, and deal with her anger which brought chaos to my world. I no longer wait for her to ask me whether I was telling the truth. A phone call I was waiting anxiously for, for most of my life, is one I now ignore. Messages I thought I would never get, are messages I don't even open. Letters to me, remain unopened.

I have spent my life fighting them off and I will spend the rest of my life fighting to maintain adequate distance between us just so that I can maintain my sanity and my me'ness. It is a fight that I would have to fight until the very end. It is a war I had been called to, and I cannot walk off halfway through or surrender

ALEX JONES

THE AFTERWARDS
BROKEN DAUGHTERS: MADE BY BROKEN FATHERS

simply because they want a way back in, bringing storms with them. At times, I am angry when I remind myself that I was left pleading my case to the law, being responsible for my father's subsequent arrest, hearings, and all that went wrong after that. I was the scapegoat, my mother's emotional dumping ground. I had every right to gain all the courage I could get together and walk away. I don't plan on returning to anything I've already rescued myself from.

I thought I needed closure. I thought I needed to understand her hatred for me in order to work through my anger for her. I thought I had to make her love me. I thought I had to do better and be better. I thought I had to spend the rest of my life making up for all the wrongs I had done. I thought I had to allow the turmoil as a way to forgive myself for the heartache and sadness my mother was flung into.

I thought I was the monster, and because of that, my ability to forgive me first will continually remind me of the fool I was for trying to understand her and absorbing all the guilt for her losses.

ALEX JONES

# THE CREDITS HAVE ROLLED

I feel that I have spent such an enormous part of my life trying to explain that removing myself from my family was not as easy as it appeared to be to the outside world. Most people who were acquainted with my mother, knew her as charming, engaging and extremely charismatic. They thought her to be beautiful, kindhearted and sensitive. Without a doubt, she had an undeniable presence about her, and attracted strangers to her. What they didn't know was that she could talk her way out of anything.

I am not denying the fact that she was intelligent, observant and well-spoken. Almost perfect in the eyes of others. In a way, she was once all that to me, and for many years, she was the center of my universe.

When I made the decision to abandon the devastation that would come as my mother, it was never as easy as I hoped it to be. It was painful and left me unable to function for days after. But, I knew that I could no longer allow her to return only

ALEX JONES

when she had a need of what I could offer her. I couldn't listen to anymore of her empty promises and false apologies. I couldn't allow her to enforce the belief in me that I needed her, and my rejecting her would leave her devastated. It had all happened before, and it was all done once or twice before.

The credits had started to roll, and instead of background music, it was done in silence. Barely noticeable, and when I was gone from her life, she barely even noticed. For almost a year, she didn't realize that I had left, for good this time. I changed homes, cities, jobs and picked up all the crumbs that led her back to me, year after year. I removed all traces of my whereabouts from social media, and I broke off contact with all family.

What our extended family saw, was a mother whose focus seemed to be on her children, and for that, I was harshly judged for walking away from her. What they saw was a woman who wasn't a victim of my father, but a casualty of my war with her.

What they couldn't know was that by impersonating a victim and commanding pity, she had inserted herself into my sisters' lives, and the lives of those closest to her. As said before, to keep them subdued and gullible, she praises them for qualities they don't have, and exaggerates their skills. Qualities and skills

ALEX JONES

she knows she can substitute and "fake it until they make it," should it be needed.

Again, when the credits began rolling, I was able to evolve back into my own self and become the person I set out to be. I was beginning to understand that my entire world was inside of me, and to find peace, I would have to be at peace with myself. With each deep breath I had taken and released, I found something inside of me that made me stronger. For the first time, I realized that I had been through much, and I deserved to be credited for a life I was choosing to live.

I got up each day and I showed up to my life. I got through it, and I saw the beauty in it. I embraced my bravery, and I noticed the beauty inside of me, and in the hearts of those who chose to encircle me. I was no longer lying in wait for the boogeyman, instead, I was counting all that was right in my life, surprised by the little things that brought endless joy.

The little steps I have taken to get me from one point to the next, were filled with moments of inspiration that led to a change in the decisions I made. Before long, I became acquainted with belly laughter, and a smiling heart. I was watching sunrises and sunsets. My days were fun-filled days, and my conversations were meaningful. It was exactly the right time to change.

ALEX JONES

## THE AFTERWARDS
### BROKEN DAUGHTERS: MADE BY BROKEN FATHERS

It was time to slow my heart down to the bad things and get it racing for all that would revitalize my life. I wasn't apologizing for loving my mother, instead, I was saying no to her. I wasn't apologizing for following my dreams, and selfishly thinking of myself. I was prioritizing that which was a part of my plan, and I was rolling the credits on toxic relationships in the process.

My imperfections were mine, and I embraced them. It was time to stand my ground and tell the truth. Life was getting simpler the older I was turning. I no longer wanted the unnecessary drama, and I loved hearing the sound of my voice. I was responsible for my joy, and only I knew the true extent of the pain I once felt.

When the credits had finally rolled, I was able to open a brand-new door to freedom.

God bless you, unbroken daughter.

THE AFTERWARDS

ALEX JONES

# IT'S GOING TO BE OKAY, I PROMISE

In The Afterwards: Broken Mothers of Broken Daughters made by Broken Fathers, I left a message for you and your mama about the unexpected emotions that engulfed me when my monster died and became my dad again. It has also shown me that mamas might be so broken by your abuser, that they begin to self-destruct.

But daughter, it gets better. Speak to mama. It's going to be okay.

The Afterwards

-        Available in hardcover, paperback & Kindle

The Afterwards: Broken Mothers of Broken Daughters made by Broken Fathers

-        Available in hardcover, paperback & Kindle

The Afterwards: Broken Daughters: Made by Broken Fathers

-        Available in hardcover, paperback & Kindle

**ALEX JONES**

Manufactured by Amazon.ca
Bolton, ON

45942514R00104